The Complete Guide to

PROPERTY INVESTING SUCCESS

The Complete Guide to Property Investing Success

Book Design and Setting by Neil Coe (neil@cartadesign.co.uk)

Set in FS Albert 10 on 12pt

First published in 2008 by;

Ecademy Press

6 Woodland Rise, Penryn, Cornwall UK TR10 8QD

info@ecademy-press.com

www.ecademy-press.com

Printed and Bound in Great Britain by Marston Book Services Ltd, Didcot, Oxon

Printed on acid-free paper from managed forests. This book is printed on demand, so no copies will be remaindered or pulped.

ISBN-978-1-905823-47-5

CONTENTS

Chapter 1

Chapter 2

Chapter 3

Chapter 4

Chapter 5

Chapter 6

Chapter 7

Chapter 8

Chapter 9

Chapter 1

Introduction

"Success is nothing more than a few simple disciplines, practised every day, while failure is simply a few errors in judgment, repeated every day. It is the accumulative weight of our disciplines and our judgments that leads us to either fortune or failure."
Jim Rohn

In these pages I will show you how to invest in property and create residual income that can eventually replace earned income. Using a few simple principles, you can grow your own property portfolio that will provide all the money you need, leaving you free to enjoy life.

I began investing in property in 1995 and have built a portfolio with my husband Dave of more than 60 to date properties worth over £10 million, with more than £2 million in equity and released cash. Property is our main source of income. Neither of us previously had a high income or any other special advantages, yet through property investing we have become financially free.

> *"Most people overestimate what they can accomplish in a year - and underestimate what they can achieve in a decade!"*
> **Anthony Robbins**

If you stop to think what you were like ten years ago, I am sure you will agree that you are now very different from the person you were then. Whether or not you feel you have made as much progress as you would like over the last decade, now is the time to resolve that you **WILL** achieve your aims and goals for a brighter future starting today and it is my aim through this book to help you.

The information in this book can enable you to retire younger and richer than you may ever have thought possible. Buying to let is ideally based on a medium to long-term investment outlook. Indeed, it could be said to be the equivalent of value investing in shares (as practiced by Warren Buffett, one of the world's richest men), which is based on the idea of buying stock that is undervalued relative to its long-term trend or prospects. This is the ideal circumstance in which buy to let property should be purchased. But the good news is if the current market does not provide such conditions, they can be artificially created in the property world (unlike shares) through **buying below market value** – which is why this has become so important.

Despite short-term corrections in prices, property has quite consistently doubled in value every 7-12 years over the last century; hence the long-term prospects for property are very positive. Of further significance for renting out property, the private rented sector is growing.

It is only since 1996 that buy to let mortgages have been available in their current competitive form and this, together with the increasing demand for rental property due to demographic factors, has provided the opportunity for ordinary people to make a fortune using other people's money. This is a crucial and unbeatable point about property investing, relative to any other business or investment. There is no other business for which you could so easily borrow 85%, 90% or even 100% to start up! This is known as leverage and is one of the key benefits of property investing. We will be developing this point a great deal throughout the book.

Although I believe there is no better business than property, I do recommend you consider as many alternatives as possible before deciding on property. You may have a very unique ability or talent, or discover a market that is about to explode! Most people at some stage wonder how to make money beyond the idea of getting a job. Each person will have his or her own individual circumstances and reasons for this. It is important to know what you really want: what your own personal goals and wishes are, and how you would like to live your life. So take time to reflect.

As well as the more obvious reasons:

- I want to invest my money to make it grow

- I want to become a millionaire

Further reasons may include:

- I aim to retire young, retire rich

- I would like to become an entrepreneur instead of working for others

- I want to prove my worth in the world, which I have found difficult to do in paid employment

- I only get paid acorns, but I am determined to grow a mighty money tree

- I find my work unfulfilling

- I have been made redundant

- I'm worried about my pension

- I have to be at home caring for young children or other dependents

And not forgetting, of course, if property investing is for you:

- Property investing excites me and I love the idea of being a property investor!

It is important to have a passion for what you do as it will be your life and you want to enjoy how you live it! I can honestly say that one of the best things for me about being a property investor is the people I meet, who are a generally fun-loving bunch. Most successful property investors have high levels of integrity too, in my experience.

Having decided that property investing IS for you, you must ask yourself whether you want to buy to let or are more interested in property development. As a property developer, you must further decide whether to let property you have developed, or sell it when complete. Or perhaps you would rather get involved in making money from property in other ways, such as by becoming a letting agent.

You can only choose wisely when you have first examined all the options and are then able to make clear distinctions between one choice and another.

The finer the distinctions you can make, the better the quality of your decisions will be.

Within the realm of property investing there is a whole range of possibilities, in addition to buy to let. One of the appealing things about property is that there is so much scope for different approaches and here are just some examples:

- You may choose to spend money improving or extending your own home, or principle primary residence (PPR), perhaps by having a loft conversion or adding a study. A big advantage here being that any capital gains arising will be totally exempt from tax. Some people choose to improve their own home as a first step to property investing, having the home re-valued after improvement and then re-mortgaging, to subsequently use the funds generated as a deposit on their first investment property. There are lots of magazines (with websites) that you can find on newsagents' shelves, aimed at people interested in improving their own homes.

- You may be attracted to buying property abroad, either to let or as a second/holiday home, often a combination of both. (A variation being to purchase a time-share property).

- You may be looking to buy a holiday home or country residence within the UK.

- You might choose to invest in commercial property. Whether large or small, commercial properties really are distinctly different from residential property, with quite different market forces operating.

- You might be interested in building your own property, or at least project managing your build (or, more modestly, an extension to your existing property). Self-building is very popular today and there is a wealth of information, including several magazines and websites, available on the subject.

- Barn conversions are very popular in recent times, for luxury homes.

- If you are keen on building, you may even consider setting up your own building company.

- You can invest in reversionary properties. This is done through a specialist agent. The arrangement involves older people selling on the equity, or part thereof, to the buyer at considerably below the property's market value, in return for the rights to stay living in the property for life - sometimes rent free. Not a good cashflow choice from an investor's viewpoint though.

- There are still potential bargains to be found by buying property at auctions.

- Or, of course, you may stick to the more basic buy to let opportunities, although even this covers a wider range of opportunities than it may at first seem.

For any form of property investing, you may wish to act singly, with a partner or as a group of investors forming a syndicate. You may seek property to buy for yourself or as a finder or agent for others. You may act as an individual, a partnership or a limited company.

The list below shows some of the finer distinctions that should be made in property investing. All of these points will be further examined throughout the book, so that you can decide what's right for you:

- Which types of property do you want to buy, and where?

- How do you want to go about buying your property? Consider how you may buy property below market value and how much time realistically you can find for this.

- How will you manage your property or development project?

- Do you want to deal with tenants yourself?

- In any area of property investing, you will find costs which may be improved on. Question everything from purchase expenses and insurance to management and maintenance costs.

- It is important to continually plan, forecast and keep your records up to date, as well as carrying out a risk assessment before each new move.

- You will need a game plan - or overall idea of what your investment strategy is for life. Know your long-term goals and your exit strategy.

- You should also be aware of your own strengths and weaknesses and the areas in which you need to develop further. Develop awareness of who you need to create a winning team.

- Finally, most successful entrepreneurs are conscious of the need to have the right mind-set for success. I began my self-education with an examination of these principles and hope you will explore them further too.

Your decisions will be based on the quality of your information. It is possible for you to build wealth through property investing by making shrewd decisions and picking your way through the minefield of possible mistakes.

I was a late starter with regard to investing, having been brought up in a financially naïve environment where money was not much discussed. In common with many youngsters, I was not bothered about money in early adulthood, as long as the ends met. As a student, my thinking was along the lines that money was something you only cared about when you couldn't get the drinks in, eat, or board the bus to college! For me, it seemed right to focus on different things at different phases of my life: first fun, then love, marriage, babies… Money could wait!

However, eventually wealth creation beckoned, and I became determined to create financial success for my family.

I became interested in the idea of how to become a millionaire, before deciding upon buy to let. It was important to me that I made the right choice for us, out of the many possibilities. The first book I read about making money was called How to Make £1,000,000 in Two Years or Less (no longer in print). The book did not give detailed knowledge on any one area, but covered a lot of options and suggestions for further reading, which turned out to be of great future benefit. It set me on a trail that eventually led to property investing.

As well as books and courses, I found monthly publications of particular use as they keep readers informed on up-to-date issues and opportunities. Newsletters on every subject abound these days particularly via the internet and can help you to stay motivated as well as informed.

I continue to attend exhibitions and seminars, both property focused and more general business events. I recently attended a very worthwhile two-day training event about Internet Marketing which was very informative. I firmly believe in the importance of recognising that there is always more to learn.

My extensive study and research also helped me consider the many possible options beyond property investing, from each of the four asset classes.

The four main asset classes are:

- Property (including residential, commercial and land)

- Intellectual property and information products (such as patents and copyright; the value of your knowledge; books, music, film)

- Business (including any goods, services or commodities traded)

- Stocks and Shares (listed on stock exchanges, or unlisted – such as private companies, angel investors)

I considered each of these areas, but decided that financial progress would be best made when starting out by focusing on just one area. Focus is an important element of success.

So what are the great attractions that property investing holds? Here are ten great reasons for investing in property:

1. Property investing can be started as a part-time, home-based business, while you may still have the safety of your original main source of income; or you may have young children at home to care for, as I did.

2. There are many ways of investing in property, so there is something to suit everyone. Property also lends itself to duplication by repeating your formula for property purchases using a simple cookie cutter principle.

3. Mortgages and bridging finance can be used to leverage your position quickly. It is easier to raise finance for a buy to let business than virtually any other type of business.

4. Capital appreciation: The biggest financial gains can be made by the increase over time in the property value.

5. You should aim for good **cash flow** from your properties, both to provide income and also a buffer against possible problems or voids. Get this right and the income from property can become your main or sole source of income, replacing other income.

6. Property investing has great potential for passive or **residual income**. It is a smart move to shift your income streams from linear to residual as this will give you the freedom to do what you really want with your time.

7. Property investing fits the ideal of not requiring you to employ others directly, thus avoiding the myriad legal complications and potential problems of being an employer.

8. Property can be a good alternative to a pension.

9. Property offers low volatility relative to many other investments such as shares. Long-term trends show that property prices double on average every 7-12 years.

10. Tax advantages: Many of the expenses involved in the running of buy to let property can be deducted from the rental income for tax purposes. When you sell, capital gains tax (CGT) relief may also apply.

Before you buy your first property, ask yourself why you are buying it and what you really want to achieve. You may be happy to own just one or two properties in addition to your own home, perhaps as part of your pension arrangements. Risk is always inherent in expanding the number of properties, as this will be likely to entail further borrowing and the higher levels of gearing can thin the profit margins. You may decide that a SMART investment goal for you is to buy just one property at first and see how that works out. Many investors buy just one or two properties, maybe with low gearing and a repayment mortgage, aiming to own them outright within 15 years thus assuring themselves of a decent pension.

A survey by the Association of Residential Landlords (ARLA) in June 2006 showed the average number of properties held by landlords as five, although this polarises between the 53% who have only one or two and the 10% who have more than 10 properties as shown in the graph below:

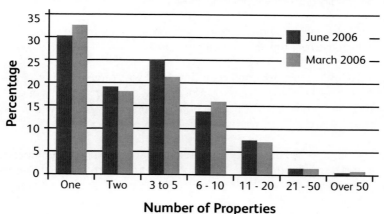

Number of Rented Residential Properties Owened

Number of Properties
Source: ARLA Survey June 2006

When we bought our first investment property, we had no idea at the time that we would eventually buy many more. You may be daunted by the prospect of aiming to own more than one property at the outset. Indeed, it is no bad thing to take baby steps when you start out. Any new venture or experience can seem like a walk in the dark; you see only a small way in front of your present position most of the time.

Our First Investment Property

As you go along, you should begin to find your way illuminated with ideas. These ideas may come from within, from contact with others and learning from their experiences and mistakes, from books, seminars, forums and other sources of information. The benefit of knowledge and tapping into other people's experience cannot be over-estimated and is an important form of leverage.

Whether you are investing alone, as a couple or within a group context, you need to tap into all aspects of your strengths in order to maximise your success. Do not be disheartened if you are working with others who are very different. In fact your differences should be viewed positively as something that will help you to achieve more. Even if you are working alone, you will need to develop a good team in some form, including your solicitor, accountant, mortgage broker, agents and others.

"Alone we can do so little; together we can do so much"
Helen Keller

Dave and I are very different in our outlooks and this has been a key factor in our success. There is synergy (like the Japanese concept of yin and yang) in all the strengths of each of us being blended into our recipe for success.

Excerpt from Dave's Diary...

Thursday 4th March, 2004:

Went to see Mary at 54E, gave her a refund that came from the council re her rent. At 11.30 am went to 15E to sign some paperwork so they can claim housing benefit. Had a viewer at 11 o'clock at 5R and 7M; had a viewer at 5 pm at 5R and 7M; took a deposit on 5R. Also went to 26S [this is one of my brothers' houses that we manage] and injected some leak sealer into their combi-boiler, because it keeps losing pressure. I also unblocked 57B drain; I bought a set of drain rods and rodded it out, because there was water coming up through the back garden whenever she ran the tap.

You can read more excerpts from Dave's Diary in Appendix I.

I enjoy the planning and administrative side of the business, while Dave is very practical. He is very well suited to dealing with the two enormous tasks of coping with property maintenance and tenants. This has enabled us to manage our own properties successfully, thus saving on the costs of having them managed, which has been a big factor in creating sufficient cash flow for both of us to live on at a relatively early stage.

This book gives practical guidance to help you find your way in property investing. As you absorb the information and insights into both my chosen way of property investing and other options, you will gradually develop the clarity to find your own niche and undertake your own property investing journey.

I wish you all the best for your success.

Disclaimer

Please note that your own individual circumstances may vary from the general examples and guidance given in this book. The book is intended for general guidance only and does not constitute mortgage, accountancy, financial, tax, or any other professional advice. Angela Bryant does not accept any responsibility or liability for loss which may arise from sole reliance on the information contained in this book.

Chapter 2

Sourcing, Analysing and Structuring Below Market Value Property Deals

"We can do only what we think we can do. We can be only what we think we can be. We can have only what we think we can have. What we do, what we are, what we have, all depend upon what we think."
Robert Collier

Over the past few years I have learnt the essential secrets of buying property below market value.

As this book reveals, there is a lot **more** to being a successful property investor in the long run than the fashionable focus on finding below market value (BMV) deals might on its own suggest. Buying properties BMV will not on its own make you a successful property investor. Running your portfolio well is as important as ever to sustainable success. Nevertheless, buying below market value can be an important element of success in today's property market.

In a later chapter Choosing Your Property we will look in more detail at deciding **which** properties to buy. Whether you are buying below market value or not, it is important to know how a given property fits within your overall strategy and goals.

But first let's consider the significance of buying below market value and then look at a step-by-step process for doing so, including:

- Financing your BMV Deal

- Sourcing properties to buy below market value

- Advertising and marketing

- Contact with clients and being a solution provider

- Researching open market values, both on-line and off-line

- Structuring the property deal

- Getting the property back onto the market at the right price

Finding your own great below market deals can take time and dedication. You may decide that you do not have the time required for this and would prefer to let others source properties for you. However, it cannot be over-emphasised that if you do so, you must always evaluate the true market value independently, so you know with certainty that the deal on offer is at a genuinely good price. If at all possible, and to avoid the added costs of using a finder, it is preferable to source your own property deals.

The Significance of Buying Below Market Value

Even people who have built up substantial portfolios in times of a fast rising market can get to a point where they feel stuck. A couple of years ago I was at such a stage myself when market conditions changed. I was determined not to remain stuck, so I made it my mission to find the right way forward. It was time to develop new tactics for a new era.

When I began investing in property in 1995, it was the beginning of a long-running upward phase of the property market cycle. Historically, in keeping with the economy in general, property prices go through cyclical phases.

As market conditions change, so you must be prepared to change your strategy. In any business, as in life generally, change is inevitable. We must evolve or die.

So, what about investing in property today:

- Have you missed the boat?

- Is the property party over?

- Is it sensible, sustainable or even feasible to begin investing in property now?

- And most importantly, do you need a different strategy than ten or even five years ago?

Despite the current market correction in 2008, prices are still high and in many areas it is difficult to find good deals where the rental cover allows for maximum borrowing. Rents should catch up with prices in the long run, but this is the key challenge in many areas of the UK today, particularly with mortgage lending rates being set at a premium.

While everyone would love to always buy BMV, finding deals that are significantly below market value can take a lot more time and effort than simply buying closer to the open market value (OMV). There are times in the market cycle when property prices may be rising steeply. At such times, if the figures work with regard to rents and you have the money for deposits but not the time to look for BMV deals, it may still be the right answer for you to buy at open market value.

A slow, flat or even falling market with media-driven fear of a crash provide ideal conditions for finding below market value deals, as vendors are anxious about achieving a quick sale.

Market falls, or 'corrections', are not a problem for the long-term property investor as prices will recover and rise in the long term. Buying below market value allows a wide margin on purchase price to value, so mitigating the risk of making a loss on the property should you want or need to sell it quickly. This margin should be adjusted in keeping with market conditions when buying.

No Money Down

Over the past few years, shrewd property investors have benefitted from being able to do "no money down deals" due to the availability of instant remortgage products. Whilst at the time of writing no lenders are currently offering the product, it is worth noting from an historic point of view and because it could become re-available at some time, so it is worth understanding how it works.

The mechanics of no money down:

If you could buy the property for a 15% discount and arrange to find the initial purchase funds from elsewhere, normally using bridging finance, you could then re-mortgage, sometimes instantly, to 85% of the open market value and pull the initial money out from the deal, thus achieving a no money down deal.

For further details about bridging finance, please visit my website at www.aquickbridge.co.uk

Here is an example of how this type of borrowing could help investors to achieve a no money down deal:

- Purchase price of property is £115,000 and open market value £140,000 (giving a discount of around 18%).

- Open market rent is £775 pcm.

- Buyer arranges a re-mortgage at 85% of open market value, which gives a mortgage of £119,000 assuming an interest rate of 6.25% at 125% rental coverage. (These calculations are covered in detail in Chapter 4: Money Matters).

- Bridging finance is obtained for the sum of £115,000 to buy the property and then the buyer switches to a remortgage immediately after purchase, repaying the £115,000 plus fees of £1,150 (at 1%) a total of £116,150, leaving a small balance in hand and a no money down deal.

How to Buy Lots of Properties with Only One Deposit

You may have a lump sum of money which is enough for one deposit, but you plan to buy lots of properties. In this case, you may consider mortgaging and then re-mortgaging using your own money, the re-mortgage money replacing the original mortgage and deposit. This allows your original deposit to be released and used again.

This could work out cheaper than using bridging finance but not necessarily, as it depends on the fees attached to the mortgage applications, of which there will be two using this model.

Portfolio Borrowing

If you already have a sizeable portfolio with sufficient equity and cashflow, you can release funds for further purchases. Portfolio borrowing can also be useful for purchases on which lenders are reluctant to lend; for example on a property requiring extensive renovation, mortgage lending may be limited to a lower percentage until the work is done. This is known as a 'retention' on the mortgage offering. If you buy property in need of refurbishment, get it re-valued after the work has been carried out. An 85% mortgage at the open market value at re-valuation could enable you to release all the cash you put into the deal, both on purchase and for refurbishment. The faster any work is carried out of course, the quicker your cash funding will be available for your next deal.

In some instances where the initial purchase price is too low for the minimum lending requirements, it may be necessary initially to purchase the property entirely with cash or bridging finance. Assuming you are confident that refurbishment or development will bring the property value above mortgageable levels, you will again be able to pull your money out at the point of re-finance.

Sourcing Properties

Many serious property investors have, over the past few years, concentrated on finding below market value property opportunities using marketing either alone or as a group, with leaflets, newspaper advertising and other methods. However, since current market conditions are indicative of this being a buyer's market, bargains are to be more easily found. I believe it is therefore important not to overlook, indeed for experienced investors to re-evaluate, buying from estate agents and auctions.

Buying from Estate Agents

Don't reject buying from estate agents as a possible avenue for finding properties below market value. Estate agents are, after all, still the first port of call for most sellers and in practice, many of the people who contact 'quick sell' advertisers already have their property on the market with estate agents. If you look for deals via estate agents, you could reach some sellers who are prepared to accept sizeable discounts before they ever approach quick sell companies, who many will only go to as a last resort.

Be aware that if you are looking for great deals through estate agents, you will be in competition with other investors who are doing likewise. It is important to establish good relationships with your chosen agents. One way to establish your relationship is to first put deals their way – give before you receive.

If you have bought a property below market value and then give it to an agent to sell, at the same time telling him about what you do and that you are a professional investor who buys and sells (or rents out, if you are looking to use their lettings department) he will be keen to put deals your way as the relationship is clearly beneficial to both of you. If you find a vendor whose property you do not wish to buy you could suggest they put it on the market with the good agent instead, who will be grateful that you put business their way.

Having established a good relationship with your estate agents, you may be able to arrange to get a surveyor's valuation done without their presence to ensure an open valuation which could be useful for the further release of equity from the property later.

Buying at Auction

I have met people for whom buying at auction is the main way in which they buy. It can be a time consuming process where you can expect a fairly high level of wastage in terms of deals you research but don't "win" at auction on the day. You may be lucky enough to find a great property deal at auction. However, if you are not keen on property development (or don't have the time), be aware that at many auction a high percentage of properties on offer may be suitable for development rather than being ready to rent. Auctions attract a lot of professional buyers and developers who you will be bidding against.

The relatively few ready residential properties that go to auction may either have hidden problems, or have so many people chasing them that the price rises to even above market value.

There is a whole array of unspoken rules about how to bid and win property at auction which you should become familiar with before raising your hand to buy! It is well worth visiting a few auctions before you intend to bid on anything. Notice where the serious bidders stand (often at the back, so few others can see them) to be as inconspicuous as possible; notice when they join the bidding (often not early) and how the professionals aim to appear nonchalant and unemotional about their bids.

Many good deals may be done either before or after the auction itself. If the reserve price has not been met during the auction for example, there can still be room for negotiation after.

If you aim to buy property at auction, be aware that completion is normally required within 28 days and also that you will be required to pay a deposit of 10 per cent of the purchase price on the day, which can be by bankers draft for example.

Joining a National Network

If you plan to source properties to buy below market value, you need to be proactive. You can do this completely independently simply by applying the knowledge gained from this chapter, if you choose. Having others to work with for support is of course always motivating and can make the difference between staying on track and losing focus and motivation. Many people I know, in practice, who achieve consistent and long-term success have undertaken further training at courses, or joined national networks or mentorship programmes.

Property networking groups, training and mentorship can provide welcome encouragement and support to those seeking below market value deals on a consistent basis.

Whether you join a support group or go it alone with the help of this book, make a start by doing some advertising and marketing.

Advertising and Marketing

Whether you plan to operate independently or join a national organisation, marketing is normally considered an important part of finding BMV deals. The cost of advertising is a necessary and worthwhile investment for finding great deals on a regular basis.

There is no fixed formula for how much you should spend on marketing but it is important to appreciate the nature and basic principles of marketing:

- You will need to spend (or rather invest) money to advertise.

- Not everyone who receives your ad will appreciate doing so, let alone read it or wish to act on it.

- Of those who do contact you, only a percentage will become deals. The number of leads you convert to deals may be anything from one in five to one in hundreds, partly depending on your criteria and required level of discount and partly on the quality of your marketing.

- It is very important to be clear what your criteria are before advertising, so that you can target your preferred market as well as possible accordingly.

- Your skill as a negotiator will also have some part to play in your conversion rate, so be honest with yourself about this and be prepared to work at improving. Most of us will improve with practice, so do not shy away from trying.

- It is essential to test and measure your results, so you can hone your marketing budget to be used as efficiently as possible:

    o   Track results for each different advertising outlet.

    o   What is your cost per lead?

    o   What is your cost per deal?

Continually review your marketing efforts and be prepared to pull advertising that's not working in favour of advertising that's producing better results. It is important to get the timing right on this, neither giving up too soon nor keeping going too long with a particular marketing campaign. Three months is normally sufficient time to see what's working and what's not.

Test individual adverts, to see which wording works best. A good way to do this is to give alternative adverts a different reference number that you can ask people for when they phone or otherwise contact you. You may also put a different contact name on alternative ads, so callers "ask for Steve" or "ask for Jessica".

The various forms of advertising that will be suitable in most cases include:

- **Business Cards:** Have business cards made up that say something like this:

    o   *"Property always wanted. Cash buyer. Fast sale. Tel: 123456"*

    o   If you wish to take leads from others who come across good deals, your card might say (possibly on the back):

    "£500 minimum paid for finding the right property in XYZ location."

Let people know what you do and what you're looking for and don't forget to take your cards with you when you go out!

- **Newspaper Advertising:** You may wish to try a small lineage ad in the local paper before going for anything more expensive. Small ads can be just as effective.

Don't be put off advertising in papers where others also have ads: this may be a positive sign, as it shows that others find it worthwhile, demonstrating a demand and also that a good response can be obtained by advertising in that paper. Interested vendors are likely to phone several, if not all the relevant ads, so just make sure that your service is as good as it sounds and better than all the rest!

People don't like fly-by-nights and will feel more comfortable dealing with someone who advertises regularly, so do persevere and understand the importance of repeat advertising.

Your advert might say something like this:

o ***"Properties bought for cash: any condition, immediate decision; no fuss; quick sales guaranteed. Freephone 0800 12345"***

You may or may not decide to get a Freephone number arranged. (Details of the various special rate numbers can be found in your telephone book).

Or try an advert that targets specific circumstances, for example:

"Mortgage Arrears? Repossessions stopped; option to stay in home. Quick cash sale, no fees. For details contact Mike: 01999 111"

Website: Consider having a website to which respondents are initially directed to register their interest. This will give your business a really professional image. Look at other similar sites for ideas about the information to include on your website. To maintain your privacy on the internet, it is best not to include your name, address or other personal details on the website.

An advantage of using a website is that you can sift the properties you may be interested in before speaking to vendors. Your website could offer a free report or other incentive, which you can point out in your advert.

For example:

"Sell your property in 2 – 4 weeks. Free report shows you how. Visit our website at www.forafastsale.co.uk

Call Answering Service: Another useful tool for sifting calls is to use an answering service with pre-recorded message specifically for respondents to your ad. Notification of new messages can be by SMS message, email or call back with remote transcription from any touch-tone telephone.

- **Yellow Pages:** If advertising in the Yellow Pages or other trade directory it may be worth paying for a boxed advert, as this will get noticed more easily.

- **Leaflets or Flyers:** These could be home produced or preferably professionally printed. The cost of getting 5,000 double-sided colour leaflets printed could be about £150 for A5 size or £200 for A4 size. One advantage of leaflets is that you can put more information on the leaflet than could reasonably be afforded for a newspaper or other advert.

- **Leaflet distributors:** You may wish to do the legwork of delivering the leaflets yourself or pay to get them inserted with the local newspaper for example, or delivered either solely or together with other leaflets. The delivery charge for leaflets would usually be between 2p and 4p per leaflet. You could advertise for a leaflet distributor, or perhaps ask a local catalogue distributor or someone you know who would appreciate the opportunity to earn some extra cash (perhaps a student, or retired person, or even a tenant). Choose your distributor carefully, as you need to feel confident they will actually deliver your leaflets as agreed. You may wish to 'incentivise' your leaflet distributor by offering a cash bonus on any deals you complete as a result of their leafleting.

- **Targeted leafleting:** A great advantage of leafleting over newspaper or other ads is that you can target the exact properties you wish to advertise your service to. This is particularly useful when you wish to target a particular neighbourhood, or even type of property within the neighbourhood, or more specifically you may target properties which are known to be for sale (this can be more or less difficult according to the area you are working in).   As with newspaper ads, it is wise to leaflet the same properties regularly over several weeks to reinforce the message.

First Contact with Clients

Your first contact with clients will vary depending on how they first heard about your business, so it is a good idea to ask how they heard about you. If they are phoning in response to a brief advertisement in the local paper for example, it may be a good idea to offer to send further information by post, which may be your leaflet, explaining more about how you do business.

When you speak to potential clients, you must be aware of why people might contact a business that offers a very quick sale at a discount to the open market value. It is important to realise that people who are truly motivated to sell their property at below market value will have reasons for wanting to do this; it is normally because they find themselves in difficult circumstances for one reason or another. They may be quite emotional about the problems they have been experiencing and will appreciate a caring attitude; they may need a shoulder to cry on. You don't need to be a salesman, but do be prepared to be a problem solver. When you speak to vendors, focus on how you can help with their problems, not on the profit you hope to make. Listen to their troubles and be prepared to be a solution provider.

Empathise with the client, take the trouble to find out and understand their reasons for wanting to sell the property. It is important to remain helpful and professional to all, as your reputation will prove important to the sustainability of your business. Offer genuine help, even if this means the deal will not come to you on this occasion. The best solution for the client may be debt counselling for example, or just a better estate agent.

It is not in anyone's interest to pursue leads where a deal would not be best for the client as the deal is likely to fall through (or fall out of bed) before completion, wasting everyone's time.

So in what circumstances is the client genuinely likely to benefit from a very quick sale and be happy to accept the discount on price, creating a win/win situation that you can be confident will proceed to completion? Here are some examples:

- The client may have financial difficulties, or be under imminent threat of repossession.

- The breakdown of a relationship may create a sense of urgency about selling up.

- The seller may have found their dream home and perhaps had a buyer who pulled out, breaking the chain.

- The property may have been on the market for a long time and the seller is simply fed up with viewers.

- Some people have personal reasons for not wanting lots of viewers as they would be subjected to by going through an estate agent. For example, if they have a handicapped or vulnerable member of the family living at the property.

- People who are emigrating or relocating to another part of the country often need to move on quickly.

- An inherited property can be an unwanted hassle for distant relatives to manage the sale through estate agents.

Deals can be **structured** in various ways according to the client's needs and I will discuss this further on in this chapter.

As well as ascertaining the client's circumstances, you need to get further information about the property. It is a good idea to keep a checklist, perhaps drawn up into a table or form, of information to be gathered during this initial contact, which should include:

- The client's name

- Marital status

- Who lives at the property

- What type of property it is (house, flat, maisonette, bungalow)

- Number of bedrooms

- Whether it has a garage or garden

- Ask the client for their estimate of the property's value and how they arrived at this figure

Let the client know that you will do your own research and will get back to them within 48 hours to discuss your findings and how you might best be able to help them.

Analysing the Property Deal

This is of paramount importance, because there is scope for error, misleading information or the withholding of information about a property's value when all you have to go by initially may be the vendor's stated estimation of the property's worth. Clearly it is not practical or economic to have every property lead valued by a surveyor, as many enquiries may turn out to be quite casual and not worth pursuing.

You need to develop a system that relies on your own research in the early stages of enquiries. You will of course want to take further steps to carefully analyse the price of any property that has serious potential to turn into a deal.

One of the first things you need to get clear about is how much profit you expect or need to make. There is little point in advertising that you buy from as little as ten per cent below market value if that is not going to provide you with the profit you require, as the quality of leads you get may be poor and much time may be wasted. However, don't expect a rush of people eager to sell to you at 30% below market value either; such deals are rarer although market conditions and direction will affect the attitude of vendors as well as your own.

Be prepared to work backwards from the figures for the profit you require and be flexible about the discount you consider if the deal suits. Take further factors into account, such as the potential of the property to sell or rent quickly, location and property type.

For example, you may get a lead for a property that, after doing all your research, you are confident you can sell on quickly for £200,000. So what might you be willing to pay for the property? Assuming it needs no work, your figures may suggest the following costs of buying and selling:

- Legal costs, in and out: £2,000

- Stamp Duty: £1,680

- Estate agents fees to sell: £4,000

- Cost of bridging finance £4,000

- Six months' mortgage payments: £5,000

- Profit required: £15,000

By deducting these figures from £200,000 you arrive at a round price of £168,000 at which you are willing to purchase the property. This is a discount of approximately 16% only to the selling price. However, remember that the selling price you are aiming for may itself be a discount to the valuation which could be £210,000. After all, you are looking for a quick sale yourself.

If you are hoping to buy to sell, it is imperative that you are realistic when buying about the market conditions for selling. Given current market conditions in 2008, buying to sell in general is not recommended, particularly on low margins. I have seen people come unstuck recently, when they buy property they cannot sell profitably due to a slow or falling market.

Whatever your plans, it is wise to buy property at least 10% and preferably 25% or more below market value, in order to mitigate the difficult circumstances of a non-rising property market or rents that are difficult to stack up against prices.

Work backwards from the borrowing you need, to see what you can afford to pay at currently available mortgage interest rates. This will be discussed further in a later chapter.

Undertake the most careful due diligence when researching property value and recognise that information supplied by the vendor about the property's market value could be misleading. Even when you have done your best due diligence, it is normally wise to have the property valued by a surveyor before a firm offer is made. Make an offer that works for you with all costs taken into account. When you put your offer forward to the vendor, you may like to explain how you have arrived at the figure you are willing to pay for the property. Then it is up to them to decide whether they want to go ahead with selling to you.

Other than engendering the client's trust that you are an ethical operator, there is no point trying to persuade the vendor to sell to you, as the deal is likely to fall through if the vendor is not certain it is the right decision for them. Remember that the idea is to find motivated sellers, to provide a solution to their problems and to produce a win/win situation.

Before you take steps to establish the open market value of a property, it is important you understand this truism:

The only value that matters is what someone is willing to pay for the property.

You may be excited that you have found a vendor who tells you their property is worth £200,000, but they are easily open to selling to you for £150,000 - 25% below market value. You may even have evidence that the property is indeed currently on the market with an estate agent for £200,000. But what is the true value? If the property has been on the market at that price with very little interest, then the price may well be inflated. When the market is falling in particular, this is common. There may be properties on the market which have not sold for over a year at the price they insist on sticking with. Even in a good market, the estate agent may have made an error of judgement himself on the price, or indeed taken instruction reluctantly from the vendor to market the property at that price. This is why comparables are so important and this is discussed more below.

You must be clear about what you are willing to pay for the property and why, given the value you place on it after your due diligence.

It is a fact of life that property valuation is always part science/part art. Your decision whether to purchase a property should be based not only on whether this is a genuinely good deal as far as such things can be objectively established but you must also appreciate the 'art' that a good property investment decision must boil down to, answering the question: ***Does it work for you?***

- How keen you are to have this property - does it fit well with your goals? (For example, you may want a property to let that is local, or you may require a property which has scope for development and adding value).

- Your attitude to risk

- The current or anticipated market forces in the area

- The availability of finance for you to take the deal on

- The anticipated return on investment, or yield the property will produce

Property Valuation

There is much you can do to research a property's value. You may be fully confident without having to do too much research, depending on how familiar you are with the location and property type and how up-to-date your knowledge is. Whether you have sourced a property yourself or if it has been passed to you by a finder, you should NEVER proceed with a firm offer on any property until you are satisfied that you have fully and independently researched the value.

I would recommend you always get a surveyor to give you a valuation of the property at some stage before making a formal offer, unless you are 100% confident of the property's value and that you know the area and type of property, as well as current market conditions, very well. This is of course a huge advantage to operating locally, you are much more likely to know the area inside out than if you buy non-locally. Even with a professional valuation, you must realise there are no cast-iron guarantees as to the price you would be able to sell for, should that be your aim. In a bad market, selling is not to be recommended for any property.

Let's now look further at tools we can use to assist in establishing property values:

On-Line Research

Obviously, you may choose to use as many or as few of these tools as you wish, or feel the need to. For properties that you have a sound knowledge of, you will have a lot less need than properties that are less familiar.

- Check the price of properties sold since 2000 at:

  www.nethouseprices.com and www.ourproperty.co.uk

A very useful, free website. Simply enter the postcode of the target property and it will give you a list of all properties with the same postcode that have sold since 2000 and what they sold for. If the target property has changed hands within this time, you may be able to see what it sold for last time. To check average prices by property type for a specific postcode, select the appropriate postcode (eg: RH12), then select 'property prices in RH12'. Select your preferred table from the menu in the top left hand corner (eg: 'compare change since 1995') and select the property type (eg: 'semi-detached'). You can calculate the house price index* for the period between purchase and now and apply this trend to the specific property purchase price. *The house price index constitutes the average selling price for the type of property sold in the area at the period in question.

- To check the details of the property on the Land Register (£3 per search) visit:

www.landregisteronline.gov.uk

Enables you to check that the property title is registered to the client and confirms the date of purchase. The price paid for the property may be available, as well as details of any mortgage lenders and others who may have a legal charge on the property. Details of charges are contained in the Charges Register, also available from the land register.

Remember though that any one piece of information is just another piece of the puzzle and you should never rely on one piece of information alone.

It is worth exploring as many pieces of the puzzle as possible to get a more complete picture.

- Another useful piece of research is to use:

www.upmystreet.co.uk

Where you can find out about the ACORN rating for the area in which the property is situated. This gives you valuable information and insights into various socio-economic factors in the area.

Hometrack Report

- One of the most comprehensive tools available on the Internet for researching property value is at:

www.hometrack.co.uk

As well as offering an up-to-date guide on UK property trends and prices by postcode, the Hometrack website enables you to use the same information system only previously available to professionals.

A Hometrack Property Valuation Report helps you to:

- Get an instant on-line valuation of a property

- Compare local property values

- Discover house price trends in your area

- Understand local property market activity

Like all tools for researching property values, a Hometrack report is useful and informative but must be treated with caution. There is no single tool that can provide us with a definitive answer.

What I find can be most useful about Hometrack is that IF your target property was previously sold only two years ago or less, the estimated current value figure extrapolated from the sold price could be fairly accurate, barring any major development to the property or area, or indeed major very recent market correction.

- The most well-known and frequently used website for agents selling properties in all areas is

www.rightmove.co.uk

Many agents use rightmove these days and it is often the first place to look for comparable properties for sale. Your target property may even be found there, if an estate agent is currently marketing it. On first contact with the client, do find out if there is an agent currently marketing the property and, if so, who the agent is and which website the property may be found at. This way you can often see the property before visiting and details such as room sizes.

Do not contact the estate agent currently marketing the property, or they may later claim that you should pay them for sourcing the property for you - which of course they did not.

Other well-used property sale sites include:

www.findaproperty.co.uk and www.fishforhomes.co.uk
Regional and specialist directories (for example, equestrian properties) also abound and can be a useful source of further area information; you can find regional directories through a search on www.google.co.uk

- Get comparables for the rental value too:

  In the course of your research, you will want to look up comparables for the rent achievable on the property. Even if you don't intend to let it out, the rent achievable will have relevance if you hope to finance the property with a buy to let mortgage which is normally the cheapest and most easily available form of finance.

  Even if you plan to sell, it is reassuring to know if the figures stack up to make the property viable for letting, as that could provide you with a Plan B should the property prove hard to sell, or perhaps to get the property through the winter if you think it would be better to sell in the spring.

Off-line Research

- Local papers are a great source of information. If you are living outside the area, you can easily find contact details of local papers for your target area and arrange to have papers sent to your home.

- Valuations by Local Surveyors and Drive-By Valuations:

  Establishing a relationship with a local surveyor could be extremely beneficial, so do consider getting a surveyor on your team. You can of course pay for a valuation on properties you are considering, but this is best reserved for those where there is a serious possibility of a deal arising.

  Another reason for using a surveyor is if there are any question marks as to the condition of the building itself - normally in the case of older buildings or where there have been alterations to the property.

Even a friendly surveyor will not spend all his time doing valuations for you free of charge, but may be happy to do drive-by valuations occasionally for free if you put paid business his way regularly enough!

- Speaking to Estate Agents:

Never under-estimate the valuable expertise of estate agents, who are immersed daily on the front line of the property market. Their input is likely to be a key piece of the puzzle when establishing the open market value of your property. You can look at comparables yourself using all the methods outlined above but, particularly if you are looking to buy to sell, it is imperative that you know how easily the property will sell in the current market and at what price you would need to pitch it for a quick sale. To realistically achieve a quick sale in a slow market, you may need to place the property on the market for 5% below the recommended open market value.

When you speak to estate agents, make it clear that you don't want the flattering reply about the property; you want the truth about what it will sell for quickly.

As mentioned earlier, if the property is currently being marketed by an estate agent, you will not go to that particular agent for advice, so there is no room for doubt about how you found the property.

Once you are satisfied that you have gathered all the pieces of the puzzle necessary to arrive at a valuation of the property, you may wish to compile this into a report for the vendor. Any written evidence you can show them as to your workings will impress them with your professionalism. The Hometrack report in particular is very visually pleasing and giving a copy to the vendor will impress them.

Your final analysis of the property valuation will of course be based on what properties are actually selling for in the current local market, rather than what they are merely being marketed at, and you should make this point clear to the vendor. The Hometrack report may show that the average property is selling for perhaps 92% of the asking price even with estate agents, so you must take that into account before deducting your required discount.

Structuring the Deal

The deal should always be structured with the client's needs in mind. During your first conversation with the client you will have gained an insight into their circumstances and wishes. Once you have ascertained the property value and decided you are interested in offering on the property, consider how you will structure the deal to suit the client's and your own needs.

There are various creative solutions that can be applied to property deals and which may be of great benefit to the vendor but it is important not to forget that, whilst these may come to seem quite natural for you with practice, the vendor may never have heard of anything other than a straightforward sale. They may feel uncomfortable or even suspicious. Their solicitor, should they wish to choose their own, may also be uneasy and advise them against it.

It is generally best if the client is willing to use a solicitor of your choosing in any case, as most investors find a pair of solicitors that work well together for themselves and the client and who are both familiar with various deal structures.

Before suggesting anything creative you must develop trust with the vendor and a feeling for whether they are likely to respond well to creative suggestions. It is particularly important if you do agree to a creative solution, that both yourself and the vendor use solicitors who are familiar with them.

Here is a brief outline of the various scenarios that you may come across, or even look for, together with some possible solutions:

Extra Fast Sale Required

Whilst the whole point of being willing to sell at a discount (certainly from the vendor's point of view) is to achieve a quick sale, under most circumstances people will be satisfied that this may take anywhere from four to six or even eight weeks to achieve. The main focus for most people will be that they are dealing with a professional investor where there is no chain to fall apart; who knows what they are doing; has finance lined up; and can offer assurance that the deal will go through quickly by normal standards.

But some vendors, perhaps because they are under imminent threat of repossession or other reasons, may require a very fast sale of as little as seven days. In this case, you must be prepared in advance and totally confident about whether you can realistically offer this. You will need to have finance guaranteed to be in place at the required speed and, most importantly, be working with a solicitor who can guarantee to work that fast. It is likely that you and the vendor will have to assist the conveyancing process by, for example, filling in the required standard Property Information Form which you should have immediate access to printing out, taking it to the client then back to the solicitor. The normal searches that are carried out as part of normal procedure when buying may have to be indemnified: that is to say indemnity insurance taken out if there is not enough time for the searches to be done.

With regard to the finance, in this case it is wise to either have cash available or pre-agreed finance lined up such as bridging finance (as discussed earlier in this chapter). It should be noted that bridging finance companies often advertise that you can get money super fast but, in practice, if they have not dealt with you before that may not be the case. If you anticipate needing bridging finance very quickly, it is probably best to get introduced to the company in advance.

Client Under Threat of Imminent Repossession

The number of people whose homes were repossessed in 2007 rose by 21% from the year before.

According to the Council of Mortgage Lenders, 27,100 homes - the highest figure since 1999 - were repossessed in 2007 and the CML warned that the number of repossessions was likely to rise again in 2008 as the credit crunch tightens. The Royal Institution of Chartered Surveyors (RICS) predicts the number of repossessions will rise by 50% in 2008.

If you have a client who is under threat of repossession, it's important to remember that they will be feeling very vulnerable and exposed and may have very scant knowledge of what options are available to them. You must be able to offer them genuine support and advice, even if this does not mean a deal for yourself. Your reputation will be enhanced by offering genuine best advice.

You must establish firmly with the client that you need to have full knowledge of all their debts. But don't take their word for it. You can double-check what secured debts there are against the property by getting a copy of the Land Registry title. Get the client to sign a straightforward letter which you will call a Form of Authority, giving you the right to request redemption statements from all lenders with secured charges on the property.

It is vitally important that you know the client's total level of debt in order to establish whether the deal will work, before solicitors are instructed. If it transpires during the purchase process that the client has more debts than you were aware of, the deal is likely to fail and be unable to complete, wasting everyone's time and the expense of employing solicitors.

You must become familiar yourself with repossession procedures in order to be of help to your client. You might not be an expert, but you must find a solicitor who is expert in dealing with repossessions to support the client (and it may be necessary for you to pay the fees for the client). You could offer them a free written guide and make this part of a targeted advertising campaign aimed at those under threat of repossession:

"phone 0800 XXXX for your free guide to stopping repossession".

Whilst lenders vary as to their exact procedures and timings with regard to repossession, general principles do apply. Gather information from the Internet and from various lenders and produce your own free guide for clients.

How you can help save a client from repossession will depend on various factors, such as:

- Whether you have struck a mutually satisfactory deal for them to sell their property to you.

  (Otherwise make alternative helpful suggestions about what they can do)

- How advanced the repossession proceedings are when you step in.

You must be prepared to act decisively and with confidence, to help the client deal with the lender and the Courts.

Firstly, of course, you must make a judgement about the client themselves particularly if they want to rent back after selling the property to you. For one reason or another, the fact is that they did not keep up payments on their mortgage. Therefore, you must ask yourself if they will pay the rent or whether they are trustworthy, should you need to make any payments upfront to stop the repossession - although this is not normally necessary unless the bailiffs are coming to evict them imminently!

If things have progressed to a point where bailiffs are booked for the client's eviction and you do make any payments, you will need a legal agreement with the client that they will proceed with the sale of the property to yourself. Again, get a solicitor on board who understands these matters. It may be necessary to get the client to sign some form of emergency exchange document, which the solicitor can approve later.

In some repossession cases, you must be prepared to go to the Court with the client and help him to put his case to the judge to try to stop the repossession, which may involve paying money over at the Court and booking an emergency hearing, using an N244 form. The Court will accept in their consideration faxed letters from both the client's solicitor and yours explaining that you have agreed to buy the property quickly.

Sale and Rent Back

Whether under threat of repossession or not, clients who need to sell their house in a hurry do not necessarily want to move out of the property, either short or long term. If this is the case and if it works for you, you may be willing to keep them on as tenants. This is sometimes known as sale and rent back. Obviously, you will need to take a view on the history of their financial difficulties and whether they are likely to be good at paying the rent.

If you do agree to allow the vendor to stay on as a tenant, make clear to them in advance what the rent will be as well as the terms of the Assured Shorthold Tenancy (AST) agreement you will use. They need to understand that, as tenants, they do not have long-term rights to stay in the property and that you will have the power to evict them according to correct procedures, for whatever reason.

It is normally wise to agree the going market rent for the property, but you may vary this according to the terms of the sale by mutual agreement.

Please note that the government has announced at October 2008, that the Sale and Rent Back (SRB) sector is to be regulated in future. This will take time to be fully instigated and until then, the extent of the impact of such regulation remains unclear. Such pending regulation is though clearly something property investors need to be aware of.

Option to Buy Back

We have looked at the client who may wish to stay on as a tenant. Some may wish to take this a step further and enter an agreement which gives them the right (but not the obligation) to buy back the property within an agreed timescale and at a pre-agreed price. This can be arranged by using an Option Agreement.

In such situations, it is vital that you employ the services of a solicitor who is familiar with Option Agreements.

Here are some key points to note about how an Option works:

- Until such time as the client exercises the Option, they will be a tenant on an AST and will pay rent. This rent may be set at a higher rate than the normal market rent, as part of the agreement.

- The Option must be secured on an amount of money, although this does not have to be large.

- If the Option is not taken up within the agreed timescale, you can offer a new Option Agreement if you wish to do so.

Example figures for an option deal:

Property OMV	£100,000
Market Rent	£550 pcm
Property Purchase Price	£85,000
Option Agreement for	2 years
Rent to be Charged	£650 pcm
Charge for Option Agreement	£650

Option with Buy-Out Clause (OBO)

A different type of Option agreement is one with a buy-out clause, sometimes known as an Option Buy-Out (or OBO). This may be attractive for both you and the vendor, particularly where the vendor needs money urgently to avoid repossession but would ideally like to sell the property on the open market at a higher price and thinks they may have a chance of doing so, given enough time.

Any deal must, of course, be attractive to both parties and you may favour an Option set up if, for example, the property would not work well as a rental property and it is not your normal strategy to buy to sell; but, on the other hand, if you do end up buying the property at the agreed BMV price it would work for you.

So this is how you structure the OBO:

- You take an Option for an agreed price (say 25% BMV)

- You pay an Option Fee to the vendor for this arrangement (usually enough to cover the arrears on the mortgage)

- You give the owner an agreed period to try to sell the property on the open market (say six months)

- If the owner sells the property in that time, they buy you out of the Option for a pre-agreed price

- The buy-out price would normally be about double the amount of the Option Fee given, so your return would be 100% on your investment

- If the client does not sell in the allotted time, you exercise the right to buy them out at the BMV price agreed

Sandwich Lease Option

This describes a situation where you get an Option to buy a property (preferably BMV) on the one hand, and on the other you get tenants who want an Option to buy the property in, say, two years time, at an agreed price. Hence the sandwich!

Rent to Buy

This term describes the situation of the tenant who wishes to have the Option to buy at a future date: the tenant-buyer. It may be applied to a sandwich lease option or to a property that you already own or buy. The rent to buy concept is useful for people who want a home to call their own, but who either cannot afford the deposit or get a mortgage for a variety of reasons at this time.

It is usual to charge more than the market rent to get good positive cash flow. This also provides a way for the tenant-buyer to effectively save towards their deposit, as the extra loading on the rent of typically £150 to £200 per month can be counted towards their deposit.

You may wish to offer an Option to buy to current or specifically targeted incoming tenants. It can also be a useful strategy in a slow market for property that you wish to sell, to offer it to tenants, as you may have a ready buyer instead of having to try and sell on the open market, as well as having the bonus of no void period while the property is on the market.

Your Option to Purchase

An Option to purchase is useful in any situation where you want the option but not the obligation to buy a property and can be used where you only want to buy a property or piece of land if planning permission can be obtained for development. Arrange an Option for one or two years, while you take steps to get planning permission for the development you have in mind. This strategy is commonly used by big developers, but can equally be used by individuals.

Joint Venture with the Vendor

A rather different scenario that may arise is that you view a property which has great potential to increase its value with refurbishment. The vendor may be well aware of this and not willing to sell the property for the amount BMV that you require, but may also admit that they simply don't have access to the funds necessary to do the refurbishment work required.

In this case, you may offer to fund the necessary work to add the value and even manage the works if you are so inclined, in return for a split of the profits. Again, you will need a written agreement which, in this case, may be a Declaration of Trust or you may get a second charge on the property. Get a solicitor to draw up a contract for you, to protect your interests. The goal may for the vendor to re-mortgage the property at the higher value after works and repay your share of profits from that, or to sell and then split profits.

Profit Share

This is where you agree to buy the property at a lower price whilst agreeing to share profits should the property sell over a certain amount. Providing the idea is attractive to the vendor, this can provide many advantages.

An example of a situation where profit sharing is useful may be where the open market value of the property is a little unclear and particularly where the vendor's assessment of OMV is substantially higher than your analysis suggests.

Effectively, this can be a useful way of calling their bluff in such circumstances. I had a situation like this myself where the vendor insisted the property was worth £500,000, but my research suggested that the property would maybe only sell for £375,000 in the current market.

I explained to the vendor that because of the discrepancy in our valuations and the difficult market conditions, as well as the expenses at such a price level, I would prefer to buy the property for just £250,000 (to keep under the Stamp Duty threshold) and profit share with him on the basis of an 80/20 profit split in his favour should the property sell for over £300,000.

Retained Equity

This can be useful where the client has a sizeable amount of equity in the property but the deal only works at a big discount which might otherwise be unacceptable to the client. This is normally used where the client wants to rent back for a while but not necessarily indefinitely. You can arrange the deal so the client retains an equity share in the property which they will get back when the property is eventually sold, or you may arrange to pay the retained equity to the vendor at an agreed future time when you expect to have sufficient funds either from increasing the mortgage or from elsewhere. Such a deal will be contractually supported of course via solicitors at the time of purchase.

The following section looks at how to approach the client on second contact, once you have the results of your research findings and have planned the deal structure.

Second Contact Call to Clients After Analysing the Deal

When you make your second call to the client, you will have all the results of your research to hand. You will need to make a judgement at this point whether to visit the client before or after discussing figures. This may depend on several factors, such as time and distance, how keen you are to secure the deal, or client preference. Ideally, it is better to meet the client face to face, but whether this is so or whether contact is by telephone initially, be ready to discuss the valuation and the solution (deal structure) you have thought of.

You should be prepared at this stage, if appropriate, to make a spread offer. If it is a straightforward purchase for example, you might say:

"After doing my own independent research, I feel that the open market value of your property is nearer to £190,000 than the £200,000 mark and my offer would be somewhere between £133,000 and £142,500, which is around 25-30% below the market value. Obviously, I would need to visit the property first and I could show you the Hometrack report and other findings when I come over."

Let the vendor know that your valuation is based on the actual selling price of properties in the area, rather than what they are on the market for.

Point out or remind the client that they will have no estate agents' fees to pay. You might offer to pay the vendor's legal fees (either in total, or perhaps up to £500). The vendor then feels they are getting a gift, as well as a caring attitude.

Try to put the above to the client as succinctly as possible and give them the chance to speak, or to think. Don't be too talkative about the minutiae of your research findings.

If you feel that a creative solution to the vendor's problems is appropriate, then it might be as well to mention your suggestions at this stage in brief – but proceed with caution to mention anything that could make the vendor feel uncomfortable or worried.

Many people will be unfamiliar with creative solutions and could be suspicious or put off, so use with caution. The client may well say they need time to think about your offer and get back to you in a few days, or a couple of weeks. You could make a note to chase them up with a call if you haven't heard from them after that time elapses, but balance your eagerness to follow up with the realisation that you are looking for motivated sellers, if they don't seem very keen.

When the client is ready, they will let you know if they are interested in proceeding further. By this stage, you will definitely want to arrange a viewing of the property and to meet the vendor to discuss the detail. Make this as soon as possible, demonstrating your commitment and ability to act quickly.

Visiting the Vendor at the Property

When you visit the property, you will want to appear professional but not slick. It is not necessary to act like a salesman. You don't want the vendor to feel intimidated. Be yourself and be prepared to build rapport.

Remember that it is their home. Be generous about the property's good points while respectfully noting areas where there may be room for improvement. Some people like to go equipped with a damp meter, tape measure, digital camera (with the vendor's permission) and perhaps a torch. Using such items during your inspection of the property may give you an air of authority and professionalism, similar to a surveyor.

Take a property viewing checklist with you (such as the one provided in Appendix II) so you can measure room sizes and take notes. You might ask the client if it would be all right to take some photographs of the property, especially if you are planning to offer it on to other investors; of course you should get the client's permission to do first.

When you have completed your inspection of the property (and the gardens where appropriate) sit down with the vendor and be prepared to make your offer. This should initially be pitched at a few per cent below your maximum, to leave room for negotiation. If the offer is rather low, or less than expected from previous telephone conversations, be prepared to apologise for the low offer but explain the reasons (for example, the property may not be in such a good condition as you had hoped and you must be prepared to say so <u>tactfully</u>).

Offer to show the vendor the Hometrack report and other supporting material that helped you to arrive at your valuation.

If a creative deal structure seems appropriate, this may have been discussed initially by phone, but now is the time to discuss that further too and show them any literature, forms or other supporting documentation you may have.

Ask them how long they would like the sale to take and discuss the time-scale you are prepared to work to. Bear in mind that you must be able to proceed as quickly as you promise in order to safeguard your reputation. This will be discussed further below.

Always give the client the chance to think and to speak. Listen carefully to everything they say and be prepared if necessary to get the story of their life, their divorce or their financial troubles in full. Remain at all times friendly but professional.

Be prepared to allow the client to decide whether they want to make a decision now or to think it over and get back to you.

Don't forget to remind them of the benefits, such as a guaranteed quick sale, no estate agency fees and legal fees paid.

Take two copies of a pre-written letter (preferably on your business headed paper) which outlines your offer, with blanks left to fill in at the time of the visit for the actual price you are willing to pay. Get the client to sign their acceptance of this if they are happy to do so. Keep one copy for yourself and give one to them.

If you strike a deal at this stage - congratulations! If you have to wait for them to think it over, be patient. If there is no deal on this occasion, remember that getting deals is a numbers game and other opportunities will come along.

Being Able to Proceed Quickly

It is extremely important that you are able to proceed quickly. The main reason after all for most clients to come to you will be the promise of speed.

One of the things you can do to speed up the buying process is to be prepared to take printouts with you to clients of the Property Information Form and Fittings and Contents Form that are standard requirements of the conveyancing process. Some clients may appreciate help in filling these in too.

Some buyers suggest they are a cash buyer and have advertising that heavily emphasises this. In practice, it is normally of little interest to your client where the money comes from - whether it comes from your own bank account, a bridging company or from a mortgage lender - as long as you can guarantee that it will come quickly! When using a lender, it is a good idea to use one where you have had some prior introduction so you are assured of their swift response. If possible, try to arrange a borrowing facility with a lender in advance to speed up individual applications.

When working with a broker, ensure that he understands your requirement to act quickly. Similarly, use a solicitor that you are confident can act quickly and make sure they are clear about the requirement for speed and can commit to it.

Getting the Property Back Onto the Market

Unless you are buying to let, or plan refurbishment or development of the property first, you will normally want to get it onto the market as soon as possible.

Opinions vary as to whether the property should be staged with furniture and this is for you to decide. Home-staging companies' charges vary but expect to pay around £150 per week for a minimum of 12 weeks. Alternatively, you could stage property with your own set of furniture. If you have storage available and plan to buy and sell regularly, you may consider buying furniture for the purpose.

You may choose to half dress a property with pictures on the walls, plants, ornaments and attractive curtains, which give a more homely feel than if it were completely empty. A friend of mine does this to great effect.

When you are satisfied that your property is ready, get some estate agents to give you valuations for the right price to put the property back on the market. These valuations will vary.

Be realistic about what some agents may say to get you onto their books, such as:

- Telling you only what you want to hear

- Telling you the value is significantly more than your estimation, or than the last agent said

- Giving you a higher value than all the other agents when they work to a fixed commission and can reduce the price later without any loss to them

- Failing to mention that the property may be slow to sell at the over-optimistic price

It is important to speak to several agents. Consider the quality of the agents and their advertising methods. Try to get as much information as possible about how many properties they sell relative to each other, and which is the most proactive and successful agent in the area. Even in a slow market you should be hoping to sell the property on within six weeks. Then you can take your profit, sit back and enjoy the fruits of your work. Or speed on to the next deal!

With my first buy to sell property I made the mistake of putting it on the market with the agent who gave me the highest valuation, which at £220,000 was £30,000 above the lowest valuation given. I later regretted this as it not only wasted time (during which I was paying a mortgage of over £750 per month) but also took the property sale into the summer lull period. Damage can be done to the saleability of a property just by being on the market for a long time, as buyers become wary that there may be hidden problems. So do allow for a conservative selling price.

I wish you every success in finding great property deals using the techniques included in this chapter. The methods outlined here will doubtless prove an indispensable toolset for your investment strategy. Once you have found your first property deal, you are in the business of being a property investor. Let's now look more deeply at what this entails, starting with the planning and risk assessment you need to undertake and regularly monitor.

Chapter 3

Planning and Risk Assessment

"The way to wealth, if you desire it, is as plain as the way to market. It depends chiefly on two words: industry and frugality; that is waste neither time nor money, but make the best use of both."
Benjamin Franklin

Essential to the achievement of solid and lasting success is to lay the foundations for wealth through careful planning and risk assessment. It is not enough to be buying property below market value. Good planning and knowledge of how to set about undertaking a risk analysis are essential to enable you to invest in property with due care and attention.

The first half of the chapter is concerned with planning and I will look at planning and getting organised, including:

- Effective use of technology

- Record keeping systems and software

- Keeping expenses under control

- Setting a realistic budget

- Lining up your team of professionals

The second half of the chapter looks in some detail at risk assessment. I will confront the risks of buying property and consider what can be done to mitigate those risks.

Planning & Getting Organised

Good systems and records will be an important part of your ability to cope as your property portfolio grows. In any business, even just the business called 'life', it helps to be well organised. When you are well organised, not only can you get more done in less time but it frees you to deal with the important things you want to be giving attention to, instead of spending all your time fire-fighting crises that wouldn't have arisen if you were better organised in the first place! I'm sure we've all at times had this experience, but being well organised helps to minimise those times. A great book I can recommend on the general subject of how to be organised is Getting Things Done, by David Allen.

I recently went to a friend's house for the evening, with a small group who were all very successful property investors. It struck me that those present were all very keen on developing the right systems that help their property business to expand easily and quickly. They were all keenly aware of and utilising technology and software to effect maximum efficiency of operations. I noticed during the course of the evening how our conversation often came back to systems: from satellite navigation, to handheld computers (which may double as phones and perhaps even have satellite capabilities), to the merits of having an office, employing others or outsourcing, and what software or customer relationship management (CRM) systems we use.

It should not be taken for granted the extent to which technology and the internet in particular enable business to operate at the speed and scale that is possible today.

A website to which you can refer your property leads can of course be a great benefit and can also be used to track your data and statistics. However, I would caution against putting your name and other personal details on such a site.

Record Keeping Systems and Software

When you have only one or two properties, keeping records and accounts for them should be fairly straightforward and can even be done manually. However, as your portfolio expands, you will need to consider more efficient systems for keeping financial and other records. A basic spreadsheet such as Microsoft Excel could be sufficient in the early days, if you plan to start at a modest pace.

General business accounting packages such as Quicken or QuickBooks offer the facility to customise the financial information to meet your requirements. With these programs you can create monthly reports containing income and expense information and compare this to the monthly budget. However, these programs are not specifically designed for investment property records.

There are a number of specific software programs aimed at property management; such software can manage very comprehensive details. You may be comfortable with the use of property management software to help you keep your property records in order although, with a small to medium portfolio, it is not essential.

From our early investing days, I developed my own spreadsheet for recording various bits of useful information for the properties, both for review and forward planning purposes. My spreadsheet for example records the date for the end of the tie-in period for the mortgage deal on each property, so that I can phone the lender to request a new special rate deal instead of merely reverting to the more expensive standard variable rate of interest.

Other things included on the spreadsheet are the full postal address and postcode, the mortgage lender and account number, the cost at purchase, approximate current value, mortgage amount, date further equity was last released, current monthly mortgage payments and the rent.

I also use a fairly straightforward spreadsheet to record our expenses for our accountant to input into our tax returns which is in keeping with the headings required for tax purposes.

As you purchase each property, you should keep a file containing all the purchase correspondence and information. You will require a second file for each property to record income and expenses for the accounts (and to keep all relevant receipts) and a third file for the details of each tenancy.

I keep several files for each property and record every financial transaction, every bit of income and every expense. I only transfer these to spreadsheets at the end of the tax year, which I find more convenient.

All receipts of course should be kept. Should the taxman wish to make you the subject of investigation, he can ask to look at your receipts and records for up to five years from the year accounts were submitted.

Do not forget to keep records of general expenses relating to the properties as well as those relating to each property.

Whether or not you prefer to adopt a high-tech approach to your business, there will always be papers and receipts that have to be kept. A filing cabinet is still a useful basic item for any business! Access to the internet is indispensable for ongoing research, for online banking (useful for checking tenants' rent payments and for transferring money between accounts) and for e-mail communications.

One of the things I have found very useful is my printer/scanner/copier (or PSC). I used to make frequent visits to my local shop or library to use their photocopier, often having to queue to copy mortgage applications and such. What a relief not to have to do that any more!

Another useful item of equipment is a fax machine, which I have found particularly relevant in helping clients who require extremely fast action to prevent repossession proceeding. My bridging clients can also fax agreements to me, so it gets a lot of use!

For matters relating to forward planning, it is wise to keep charts and also to keep a calendar and diary for appointments. An electronic personal digital assistant (PDA) is worth considering and can be synchronised with your calendar in Outlook. Dave still prefers to note appointments that have been or need to be made in his diary, for such things as the annual gas safety checks due for each property.

> ### Excerpt from Dave's Diary...
>
>
>
> **Tuesday 20th April, 2004:**
> Attended five gas tests with Tom Bell. While I was at 5R I mowed the lawn for them and while I was at 2R I painted the living room for them. Also at 6 pm, I went to see a washing machine, which was for sale for £40 - I got it for a spare.

When you begin investing in property, it is essential that you open a bank account that is dedicated to the investment property or properties. This will make it clear that this money relates to the business, which in turn will help you to:

- Cross-check the figures to keep your accounts intact

- Clarify the cash flow position of the business

- Make predictions about the future profitability of the business based on the historical data

If you feel that you would benefit from further general business training or advice, you may find it locally at subsidised rates through the government's business link initiative. Details are available at www.businesslink.gov.uk

Keeping Expenses Under Control

The ability to keep expenses down and keep your finger on the pulse of your financial position becomes increasingly important in any business as the market hardens or matures. Buy to let mortgages have only been available since 1996 and while it was relatively easy to make money for those 'early to the table', it has become increasingly hard over the years since.

Over time, it seems that pressure on profits has come from all sides: competition from other landlords, increasing regulation demanding more expense and the credit crunch leading to upward pressure on mortgage rates and downward pressure on property prices. Only the strong will survive - the strong being those who both buy well and manage the properties effectively, keeping expenses and voids to a minimum.

Keeping expenses under control is a key area that can make or break the success of your business. If you have not developed good budgeting skills in your own life, then you are not likely to do so in your business. Like any skill, you can improve with learning and practice. There are many books available to give general guidance and advice in this area. I enjoyed reading Alvin Hall's book   Your Money or Your Life. If you think you need such advice, then you probably do!

Although it must be accepted that you can never fully control expenses, left to grow out of control they can soon overwhelm all areas, wiping out profits.

Be constantly on the lookout for ways to try and keep expenses under control in all aspects of the business, including:

- Buying property cheaply

- Keeping all purchase costs and fees low

- Getting a good deal on the mortgage and insurance

- Spending the minimum required to make the property suitable for letting at the best rent achievable without delay

- If the property is to be sold, make sure you keep costs within the budget set for refurbishment, advertising and selling

Expenses extend to all areas of life. Maybe you can think of some right now that could be redressed? Here's a tip: look at your bank statement (online if possible) right now and consider all the things you spend money on, paying particular attention to standing orders and direct debits. Some are payable annually, or quarterly, so don't miss anything by only looking at last month's paper statement. Ask yourself, do you really need them all?

It is too easy to set up a direct debit or standing order which is forgotten a year later by the time it's payable again, sometimes at a much higher rate than the first 'discounted' payment. Do you still read that magazine, or still want to belong to that organisation that sends you unread newsletters and emails about meetings you never go to?

The question of how to keep expenses down should never be far from your mind. Remember that it is the little disciplines, practiced daily, that can make the difference between fortune and failure.

Setting a Realistic Budget

You will need to anticipate all the costs involved in your property project and set a realistic budget. I would normally estimate my costs to be around £2,500 at purchase of a property costing around £150,000. Further to this, I would look at the itemised expenses and try to reduce costs wherever possible.

Appendix III provides a template of a budget analysis for a buy to sell project.

Basic costs that will need to be considered include:

- Solicitor's fees

- Stamp duty on the purchase (for properties costing £125,000 or more)

- Lender's fees for arranging mortgage (and broker fees where payable)

- Insurance costs

- Mortgage fees that will need to be shouldered until the property is occupied by a tenant

- Costs of advertising the property to let, or letting agent's fees

- A detailed analysis, if applicable, of the cost of works should be further undertaken

- Contingency money should be set aside to allow for margins of error in all the above calculations

What's Your *Modus Operandi*?

For tax purposes, you need to be clear about whether you are buying to let or buying to sell, as the tax treatment is very different for each. In practice, the distinction can become blurred. You may buy a property with the intention of letting it out but end up selling it within a short time. Conversely, you may normally buy to sell but let a particular property out for a while (perhaps because of a slow winter market). Regardless of whether the property was in fact let out during the period you owned it, the taxman is likely to take a view on whether you bought to let or to sell, depending on your general modus operandi.

The distinction between buying to let and buying to sell is further blurred within the following areas, which normally come under the scope of property development:

- Renovation

- Refurbishment

- Conversion (often to flats)

Many buy to letters as well as those who buy to sell, choose to purchase properties that offer opportunities for adding value by the above methods. Adding value to a property can enable you to free up some of the money that you originally invested in the property. A quality buy to let lender will enable this to be done easily and without penalty, normally after six months of ownership. You simply arrange via the lender to get the property re-valued and increase the mortgage accordingly. This money can then be used as a deposit on your next project.

Buying to sell may suit you on occasions if you wish to raise capital quickly. It may be also be best to sell property that has been bought to develop but is unsuitable for letting out, or where there is no rental demand. But if the property in question is viable for letting out, I suggest that it may well be best to keep and do so.

It makes sense to stay on the effortless, **long term** 'up escalator' of rising property prices by holding all the properties you possibly can, always assuming good cashflow which is a must. Remember that despite any short term market corrections, history does show in the long term that property prices double on average in the UK every 7 to 10 years.

With the buy and hold policy of buy to let you will, over time, build up a number of properties, and get the twin benefits of income and capital appreciation. Every time you sell a property, you start again and kill the goose that lays the golden egg. There is much less scope for passive income, more risk especially in a slow or difficult market, and more work in refurbishing and development than most of us would like to undertake serially for life!

Lining Up Your Team of Professionals

In order to invest in property you will need to work with various professionals. This should be a very positive experience and help you to feel supported.

Here are some tips for finding good people to work with:

Solicitor or Licensed Conveyancer

Lenders' rules vary as to whether they will accept a licensed conveyancer to act in the purchase of a property, either alone or in tandem with a solicitor, or whether they will only accept a solicitor perhaps in a practice of at least two solicitors which are on their panel of acceptable practices. You will need to ascertain the lender's rules on this before choosing the professional who will act for you in the purchase of your property.

We preferred for some years to use a local, sole conveyancer with whom we built up a good relationship over the years. However, she has since retired and we now use a solicitor. Because the conveyancing firm was small, the service was very personal and communications quick and direct. One of our lenders accepted our conveyancer acting alone, another lender insisted on a firm of solicitors to work in tandem with her on their side of the work. With some large, centralised firms of solicitors you can be 'passed around' and dealt with by a different person each time, left on hold on the telephone; communications can be slow and impersonal. Of course, each practice will differ and it is a good idea to get a personal recommendation. I have now found a solicitor who is competent, accessible, efficient and able to act quickly.

Obtaining quotes initially will allow you to compare prices and also have an insight into how friendly or efficient they are in their services. Ask for a breakdown of what the fee includes, so you can be sure to compare like for like. If you are looking to buy outside your local area, you will have to decide whether to employ a solicitor in your own area or the area of the property being bought.

Conveyancing can now be organised online. Web-based services are often fixed-fee, and you can also check on the progress of your case at any time. Some websites additionally offer a guide to the process and normally expected timescales.

You can also find a solicitor online. www.lawyerlocator.co.uk and the Law Society's spin-off www.solicitors-online.com both have search facilities.

Accountant

It is not compulsory to have an accountant. If you only have one or two investment properties it is not too difficult, with carefully kept records, to calculate your own annual figures for your tax returns.

However, with any but the simplest of situations, it is worth having an accountant as their advice can be invaluable and can easily save you more than their fees. Your accountant can be one of your most valuable professionals and it is important to choose one that you are happy with and who understands the particular nuances of property investment. You may find an accountant through personal recommendation, preferably from another successful property investor. You may search online for an accountant at a site such as www.accountantbrokers.co.uk, which also has links to search for an independent financial advisor.

I did not have an accountant for the first two or three years. I had several reasons for deciding to get an accountant when I did, one of which was that my mortgage lenders began to request my accounts from the accountant they assumed I had. At the time that Dave was planning to give up his day job, we were informed by our lender that they would require three years' accounts from a chartered accountant to continue allowing further borrowing when he became self-employed. (The rules are more relaxed these days). When we set up a limited company to buy some properties through, we needed to have an accountant for that as a legal requirement.

Do not expect to get entrepreneurial advice from your accountant to help make business decisions such as whether to take a particular risk, or whether to expand the business rapidly. If he wanted to be an entrepreneur, then he wouldn't be an accountant! However, an accountant is very useful if you need to know the specific tax or other implications of any particular decision you take. You may have an accountant who specialises in property companies or even invests himself. If so, that can only be a good thing but remember his experience may not be completely relevant to yours, and in the end you will need to make your own decisions.

Any advice given will normally come with a price ticket - you must remember that. However, if you have an accountant who offers you great suggestions or advice for how to save money or tax, he will be worth his weight in gold.

Furthermore, with respect to getting your accountant to help sort out your end of year accounts and tax returns, you should realise that the more clearly you can present the information - in near complete form, preferably - the less the accountant should need to charge you for services. I type up my accounts for each property and a general accounts sheet at the end of the tax year, in a form that follows the categories used on the tax return forms so that the figures can be easily entered once the accountant has checked them and my accountant's bill stays low.

Estate Agents

If you do buy property through estate agents, be friendly by all means but do not try and over-sell yourself or offer bribes. In my experience, the only way to treat estate agents is with mutual professional respect. They will soon know if you are a serious buyer, in a position to proceed, who doesn't procrastinate or waste their time. One thing that estate agents are often most interested to know is: "Who is your financial advisor, or mortgage broker?" You should get one - see the section below.

I will look at dealing with estate agents in more detail, in the chapter on buying property.

Financial Advisor/Mortgage Broker

As mentioned above, estate agents may want to know who your financial advisor is, particularly when you come to place an offer on a property, as they will want to feel comfortable that you are a good buyer: a serious person, in a position to proceed.

It is normally a good idea to use a broker when choosing a mortgage, for several reasons. They have the resources to quickly scan all lenders and rates available, which are continually being updated. They often have access to favourable rates and deals with lenders that are not available to direct applicants. They can also help to fill in the application form and offer advice as to the verification documents that different lenders will require to see.

There are many choices for finding an independent financial advisor or mortgage advisor/broker. I have found very good advisors. A year ago, one advisor analysed my property spreadsheet and suggested a great idea for restructuring the finance on a dozen of my properties, to release a big chunk of equity in a way I had not realised was possible. This enabled me to move my business forward onto a new level and to offer bridging finance to others through my company www.aquickbridge.co.uk

A very experienced mortgage advisor who is used to working with investors may even be able to help with ideas for structuring your deal. It is well worth choosing your professional team carefully. To use a mixed metaphor - it is not just a question of who you know, but what they know! Ask for recommendations from other property investors.

Finally, as with all professionals, choose a broker who has time for you and who you get on with. Using a mortgage broker is further discussed in the chapter on choosing your mortgage.

Networking with other Property Investors

Networking is not only fun, but a fantastic way to speed up your own education about property. I only wish I had started sooner myself.

The London based Property Networking Club for example has branches throughout England. There are many property networking clubs to choose from and locally based groups such as the Ipswich Property Network can be the best choice. These networking groups hold regular meetings and are very well attended.

It is a good idea to join a landlord's association, whose role is to keep landlords informed of issues relevant to your business. I belong to the National Federation of Residential Landlords. As well as having a help-line and various discounts available to members including on buildings insurance, the NFRL has regular members' meetings with informative speakers and further information available, as well as a chance to network with other landlords.

For those who wish to link up with others for their property business, networking can offer a useful opportunity to find like-minded people interested in forming an investment group, syndicate or property company. Obviously, normal precautions and diligence should always be applied before getting into any form of joint ventures, regardless of whether that is with the person running a group or a stranger off the street!

Risk Assessment and Analysis

Risk assessment involves analysing the figures in any project or business and facing up to possible difficulties that may be encountered. Ask yourself how your business could cope with such circumstances, or how you would at least attempt to effect damage limitation. Many problems can be mitigated through creative thinking and good management.

You will have a unique attitude to risk and this is your prerogative to decide. Essentially, risk assessment is about using our sense of judgement to decide on best action. Take a moment to ponder the meaning of having good judgement. It is so essential – having it is like having satellite navigation to guide us to success; without it, we are lost. So what does it mean to have good judgement? Where does it come from? Part experience, part learning, part commonsense – that uncommon quality!

I found sayings abound on good judgement and would like to quote a few here, while we ponder the flavour of it:

- "Knowing a great deal is not the same as being smart; intelligence is not information alone but also judgment, the manner in which information is collected and used." **Dr. Carl Sagan** (American Astronomer, Writer and Scientist, 1934-1996)

- "Success in life is the result of good judgment." **Anthony Robbins**

- "Nothing is more difficult, and therefore more precious, than to be able to decide." **Napoleon Bonaparte**

- "Good judgment comes from experience. Experience comes from poor judgment." **Will Rogers**

- "It is with our judgments as with our watches: no two go just alike, yet each believes his own." **Alexander Pope**

Developing the skills involved in risk assessment and analysis leads us to the application of good judgement, which leads to success.

Bear in mind that your risk assessment should always take into account your current financial position. It is generally a good idea to have enough money put aside to cover at least three months' expenses according to your situation (including the mortgage payments and other expenses for any investment properties, as well as personal living expenses).

Don't forget to allow 'margins of error' around all estimations of income, yield and so on in a negative direction, as well as around all expenses and costs in a positive direction.

Before the thought of all these risks makes you think of selling up, it is important for you to recognise that is not a good idea. It is not the time to sell when things are going wrong! Stay committed to the long haul with your properties and always aim only to sell according to your original game plan. I hope the following explanation of why we wouldn't sell our properties in a market downturn will help convince you of the wisdom of holding onto your properties through thick and thin.

Why We Wouldn't Sell Our Properties in a Market Downturn

This section was originally written in 2005. My views have not changed since and indeed I am continuing to buy property today, in the second half of 2008.

I have often been asked whether we would consider selling our properties if property prices were to crash. I can tell you the answer immediately and categorically is "No!"

I have made my properties my life. I have burnt my bridges behind me and I am totally committed to the continued success of my property business. This is one of the secrets of success - if you truly believe in something, go for it wholeheartedly and don't let the circumstances and storms around you change your mind.

The most successful investors in both property and shares have adopted a long-term hold, or even a 'never sell' position. Warren Buffet is one of the world's most successful investors in shares and his philosophy has been never to sell.

The Duke of Westminster holds a fortune in land and property – 'hold' being the operative word. Dolf de Roos, who I have met in person, aims to never sell property. The best way to accumulate substantial wealth is to accumulate property: accumulate, accumulate, accumulate!

I am not unhappy if property prices fall at some point, because there will always be some upside for the wise property investor. The property market, like the stock market, will inevitably have some correction of prices at certain points. This will take the hot air (or unsustainable pace of price rises) out of the market and should be regarded as a healthy part of long-term growth. Of course, there will be bargains to be had at such times too!

Here are some cautionary notes for the faint-hearted, who may be considering panic selling in the event of a crash. Seller beware:

- The expenses involved in buying and selling properties are quite substantial and for properties that have not been owned long will be more likely to substantially impact on any capital gain. Properties that have been owned longer will have had more time to appreciate in value.

- If you did attempt to panic sell in a crashing market, you would be wading around in a financial blood bath, in as much as you would have to make all sorts of concessions to buyers (many more sellers than buyers around meaning that buyers can be choosy). In a strong market you would not have to do that. The property would take longer to sell than in good times and since it is normally advisable to have the property empty when trying to sell, you would have to support the mortgage yourself.

- In a period of market correction, some landlords are bound to sell and there will also be a slowdown in the number of new investors. This is a good thing for landlords who stay the course, as fewer rental properties lead to upward pressure on rents.

- A falling market can provide good buying opportunities for the serious investor, as desperate vendors are more willing to accept big discounts in such times.

- The long-term trend in property prices is always up. The cycles, ups and downs which may seem so big and bumpy in the present, appear much less dramatic when viewed in the context of the long term.

Our 2nd Investment Property

The Main Risks of Buying to Let

*"Behold the turtle. He makes progress only
when he sticks his neck out."*
James Bryant Conant

Problems that can arise and which you need to be prepared to face could include:

- Interest rates rise

- Rents drop in the area

- You suffer void periods

- The tenant stops paying the rent

- Legal disputes

- Failure to comply with statutory safety guidelines

- Large maintenance needs arise at the property

- The capital value of your property could fall

I will look at each of these risks in turn and consider what measures can be taken to mitigate the risks.

Interest Rate Rises

Every situation has its plusses and minuses. When interest rates are rising, there will always be some who unfortunately cannot cope with their increased mortgage payments and this leads to a rise in repossessions. This is particularly prevalent at the moment, with the number of repossessions rising steeply over the last couple of years. A successful investor should be able to mitigate against interest rate rises, by fixing their mortgages when appropriate, not over-gearing (more about that later) and by buying at the right price.

You may have the opportunity to help some of those less fortunate who are being threatened with repossession, by buying their house below market value (as discussed in the second chapter) and allowing them to rent back their home. One of the reasons why it is particularly hard for some to cope with rate rises is because the rate they are paying may be loaded (added to) due to a poor credit rating.

If you and your advisors believe that interest rates are likely to rise, then fixing the interest rate on your mortgage will ensure that any future rises will not be a problem for you, during the period of your fix. Ask your lender or mortgage broker about fixed interest rate deals, which may be available for anything from one to ten years (or even more).

If you are affected by rising interest rates, for example by mortgages that are not fixed and cannot be changed without redemption penalties applying, it may be possible, if local conditions permit, to increase rents to offset the increased costs on your mortgage payments.

At the time of writing in October 2008, the government have taken control of the decision to cut the base interest rate by 0.5% to 4.5% in an effort to alleviate the credit crunch, with further rates cuts expected. It is of course up to banks to follow this with a cut in their own interest rates, which are normally between 1.5 – 2% above the base rate. Some lenders rates are set by Libor however and this is further discussed in Chapter 5.

If interest rate rises are squeezing your profits, take extra care to review all expenses and make cutbacks wherever possible.

Rents Drop in the Area

If you encounter the problem of downward pressure on rents, you need to face up to the realities. Downward pressure on rent is most likely a sign of market saturation - in other words, there are too many landlords chasing too few tenants.

What can you do?

Firstly, a principle you must adopt as a matter of course is to be a good landlord. If you have tenants that are happy to stay in your properties long-term, they are not likely to question the rent remaining the same and may not even be aware of sensitive market information if they are not looking to move. It must be stressed though that you should regularly review your rents to ensure they stay in line with local rent levels, including the Local Housing Allowance (payable to tenants eligible for housing benefits). Current LHA rates should be available on your local council's website. You may be missing out on higher potential rents that you are simply not aware of. Make it a habit to check regularly.

If you do have to lower rents between tenancies, don't panic. Analyse your figures and, again, review expenses. It is possible that you can afford to take a cut in rental income in the short term, knowing that things will improve eventually.

Another alternative is to consider whether any of your properties can be converted to HMOs – houses of multiple occupation. HMOs and taking LHA tenants can increase your income substantially and are discussed in more detail in a later chapter.

Void Periods

Realistically, even in good market conditions, it is wise and usual practice to budget for one month's rental void per annum.

Particularly when you first purchase your investment property, there will normally be a period in which you need to set the place up for tenants and arrange to either advertise and vet tenants yourself or get an agent on board to do so.

Less favourable supply and demand factors could mean it becomes more difficult to let your property and you suffer longer void periods as a result. Being able to attract and keep tenants must be your top priority.

Be prepared to review the rent you are asking, as this will be a related issue.

Review and revise your advertising strategy. If you use agents, you may wish to get more than one agent to advertise the property. Be more creative and assertive in your own advertising. When tenant supply is high, a simple card in a local newsagent may be sufficient, but when conditions are tougher be prepared to place a paid advertisement in the best local paper (this should cost less than £20, even for a boxed advert) and consider advertising on the Internet.

We let out most of our properties now through the local council which saves completely on advertising and assures low voids as there is always an urgent demand from the desperate families we help to house. This is also discussed further in a later chapter.

If you are seriously worried about possible voids, you might consider taking out rent guarantee insurance that protects against loss of rental income. If you use a letting agent, their service package may include a rent guarantee element - ask. This type of insurance costs about £300 a year to cover £10,000 rental income and it can be offset as an expense against tax.

The Tenant Stops Paying the Rent

A minority of tenants may cause problems and this is a form of risk that will be looked at in some detail later, in the chapter dedicated to Managing Your Tenants.

If you are building a portfolio, sooner or later you will come across a tenant that doesn't pay the rent. Nearly all letting agents and long-term landlords will have had this problem.

You must be prepared to accept it as a fact of life that buying to let involves having tenants and tenants occasionally stop paying the rent or behave otherwise in ways that mean you will have to take steps to evict them. The legal framework for this is fairly straightforward and will be looked at in detail.

The assured shorthold tenancy (or short assured tenancy in Scotland) provides a legal framework that supports landlords to take back possession of their property from tenants in a fair way. How to do this will be looked at in detail in a later chapter.

Legal Disputes

Legal disputes may crop up in a number of ways and could be expensive and lengthy, though thankfully that is quite rare. Dealings with the Courts arise most often in relation to you giving notice to quit to tenants who are not paying the rent. This does not necessarily require you or the tenant to appear in Court, and is usually quite quick and straightforward.

Other legal disputes are a lot rarer, such as a landlord suing a letting agent. Or a tenant may sue his landlord because he has been injured at the property, for example. Some such events may be covered by insurance. But it is also wise to have a contingency fund that includes an allowance for costs of this nature.

Details of how to deal with evicting tenants are covered in Managing Your Tenants. It is not normally necessary to involve solicitors in evicting tenants, though you may wish to seek legal advice should other more complex disputes arise.

Large Maintenance Needs Arise at the Property

One of the great attractions of property investing of course is that property is 'as safe as houses'. Yet when you are new to anything, it can seem scary. When I began investing in property, one of my fears was the idea that the roof might blow off!

Some forms of risk are appropriate to cover with insurance. Buildings insurance is in fact compulsory, so there's no danger of you not being covered for most major catastrophes (which are extremely rare). So if the roof does blow off you should be able to claim the cost of a new roof from the insurance. (I have never had a roof blow off yet!)

The chapter entitled Choose Your Mortgage and Insurance includes a further section on insurances that are available for your investment property business.

Statutory Safety Guidelines

As a landlord, you must recognise your statutory and moral duty to comply with all regulations designed to protect the safety and basic rights of your tenants. Failure to do so could result in fines or even criminal proceedings.

It is worth noting that these are continually being updated and added to by the government and this is one reason why it is a very good idea to belong to a professional landlords association, as they work to keep you informed of these updates.

The list below shows the main areas of safety measures that must be complied with, together with links for further information:

1. Gas Safety (Installation and Use) Regulations 1994/8: This regulation came into force to help afford tenants protection from death by carbon monoxide poisoning that can be caused by gas appliances not being in good working order. It is a requirement that all gas appliances in rental accommodation be checked by a CORGI registered engineer annually and a landlord's gas safety certificate will be issued upon satisfactory standards being met. For further details about gas safety requirements and to find a local CORGI registered gas engineer, visit the CORGI website at: www.corgi-gas-safety.com

2. Smoke Alarms (Building Regulations 1991): All properties built after 1992 must have mains controlled, inter-linking smoke alarms on every floor of the property. It is in any case law that tenanted properties have a smoke alarm fitted. It is a good idea to have a clause in the tenancy agreement stating that tenants should take responsibility for checking the batteries in the alarm every three months.

3. The Furniture and Furnishings (Fire & Safety Amendment) Regulations 1998: All upholstered furniture (including sofas, beds and more) must have a label to confirm it meets the necessary standards (BS7177) for fire safety. Further information available at http://www.dti.gov.uk/ccp/topics1/guide/furnitureguide.pdf

4. Electrical Equipment (Safety) Regulations 1994: Under these regulations, landlords have a legal obligation to ensure that all electrical appliances and works they supply are safe for tenant use. A CE label must be marked on all appliances supplied. Correct plugs and fuses must be fitted and used. If there is an accident and a tenant dies you, as landlord, could face imprisonment for exposing them to unsafe appliances. (For further information, see the www.hmso.gov.uk website).

   From 1st January 2005, people carrying out electrical work in homes and gardens in England and Wales will have to follow the new rules in the Building Regulations 2004. The new regulation of electrical works is aimed at curbing the unacceptable number of deaths, injuries and house fires caused by faulty electrical installations. The changes bring England and Wales further into line with Scotland, where Building Regulations already address electrical safety issues.

Minor jobs like replacing sockets and light switches in low risk areas will not be affected. However anyone thinking of, for example, carrying out notifiable electrical work in kitchens, bathrooms or outdoors or adding new circuits to any part of their house will have to get Building Control involved, or get the work carried out by a suitably qualified electrician who is registered for Part P regulation work. If you are not sure whether work is notifiable, you should check with your Building Control Service.

The ODPM leaflet New rules for electrical safety in the home, explains the options and how to go about finding a competent person in your area.

5. HHSRS: Part I of the Housing Act 2004 brings into law the Housing Health and Safety Rating System (HHSRS), which will replace the housing fitness standard. The concept of unfitness will be replaced by an assessment as to the extent to which a house is free from hazards to health and safety. There are 29 hazards to be measured in the new system.

   Whilst these standards are applicable to all properties, there is a requirement in particular for HMOs to be tested for licensing purposes.

   Further details may be obtained from The Chartered Institute of Environmental Health at www.cieh.org.

6. Another recent regulation for landlords to be aware of is the requirement for an Energy Performance Certificate. As from 1st October 2008 an EPC will be required at the commencement of each new tenancy, the certificate being valid for up to ten years. EPCs are also part of the Home Information Pack requirements.

   For further details, see www.homeinformationpacks.gov.uk/consumer/17_Energy_Performance_Certificate.html

The Capital Value of your Property could Fall

Property prices can go down as well as up, just as with any investment, even though property is more stable and reliable than most other investments, hence the saying "as safe as houses". Temporary glitches in property values will be only hypothetical, as long as you hold the property. Capital appreciation in the long term is certain, based on the evidence of any ten year period over the last hundred years!

It is most important that you do not panic about any problems, as this could lead to rash decisions. Particularly in respect of falls in capital value, you must be aware that while property prices will rise in the long term, such progress will not be completely smooth at all times.

If you believe prices are set to crash, you may decide to hold off making any new investments until you believe that prices have stabilised. However, even in this scenario, other factors should be taken into account, such as the availability of buy to let mortgages. What would you do if property prices were falling, but rents were rising, yields and tenant demand good but the availability of decent buy to let lending shrinking fast? I would continue to buy, having faith that my property's value would still increase in the long term, if I thought future funding could be a bigger problem. This is what we have seen in the credit crunch of recent months.

Another factor which we explored earlier is that in a slow or falling market there will be more desperate sellers willing to sell at a bigger discount than in good times. And who knows where the bottom of the market lies? Nobody does in truth, so is it really wise to wait for it to arrive?

Current and Long-term Trends in Property Prices

Despite the doom and gloom portrayed by the media during periods of market correction, over the last 30 years the growth in prices of UK residential properties has averaged at least 7 percent growth per year, and some experts quote more. Selling property in a downturn is often a mistake. Property is best regarded as a long-term investment as prices always rise in the long-term. Any low points will inevitably appear as a glitch in the longer run.

There are several well documented house price indices that will allow you to keep a finger on the pulse of house prices, including the Halifax, Nationwide, OPDM and rightmove; the latter offers a monthly report comparing data from all four indices, as well as looking at regional trends, I would also recommend signing up for my newsletter at www.propertyinvestingsuccess.co.uk to keep up to speed with the current market as well as receiving further tips on a monthly basis..

In the next chapter, we will look in more detail at understanding the money matters - the actual figure work and equations you need to get to grips with as a property investor.

Chapter 4

Money Matters

"The poor and the middle class work for money. The rich have money work for them."
Robert Kiyosaki

The first financial step in your investing success is to find money for the deposit on your first investment property. If you are just starting out, it may surprise you to know that even those with 10, 20, 40 or more properties can still struggle at times to find the answer to the question:

"Where will the money for this project come from?"

Successful property investors do not normally have excessive amounts of cash. When a great opportunity comes along, inevitably the window of opportunity is brief: vendors are willing to sacrifice getting a higher price for their property if the buyer can promise to move quickly. If you don't, or can't move quickly, someone else will.

So you need to know how to get hold of money and get hold of money quickly! This need not necessarily be your own money. The less of your own money you use the better. Learning how to make full use of other people's money will help you to achieve much more in a shorter time than you could otherwise dream possible.

Using other people's money whenever possible is the fundamental basis of leverage; and using leverage is one of the fundamental principles applied by most successful millionaires. In this chapter, I will explain the principle of leverage and its benefits to property investors. But first, let's consider how to get hold of some money to begin with.

Any decision about where to find seed money for your first investment property will be a personal one. You may wish to seek professional advice before going ahead, but do bear in mind that the advisor may have their own bias towards a particular form of investment or strategy. In the end, the responsibility to make a decision will be yours.

As individuals, it is important that we recognise the difference between good and bad debt. Borrowing money to spend on consumables or depreciating assets will reduce your wealth and should be avoided at all costs. On the other hand, borrowing for investment in properties that will appreciate in value by more than the cost of borrowing can increase your wealth, but even then a positive cash flow situation is essential to success. Don't be a victim of debt: use money instead of allowing it to use you!

As a reflection of how my own views have gradually changed since I began to invest years ago, I'd like to take a look first at the more cautious approach to money and then take this up a gear at a time. It is for you to decide where you feel comfortable on this continuum and recognise that your views may change over time. Handling money is a skill and, rather like the skill of driving, it is best to start slowly until you are sure of your ability to go faster!

Using Savings

Some investors will have savings and be looking for better returns than offered by a savings account. The following charts illustrate the far greater growth achievable by investing in property at an average compounded growth rate of 15% per annum, than by leaving the money in the bank where you may only get 2% interest per annum. Furthermore, the illustration given here is before adding leverage in the way of a mortgage, which will greatly multiply the growth potential as will be revealed in this chapter.

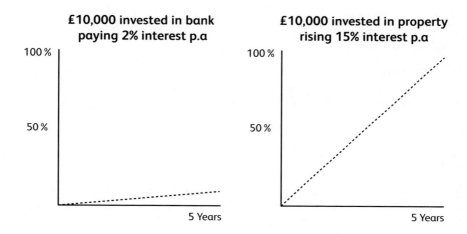

We began investing in property after paying off the mortgage on our home, in 1995. With hindsight, it now seems financially naïve to have spent ten years paying off our fairly modest home mortgage followed by a period of building up savings. However, it encouraged us to develop financial self-discipline and frugality which helped to provide a solid foundation for future success. Also, buy to let mortgages were not available before 1996, so it would have been difficult to begin sooner than we did.

Using Money from Badly Performing Investments

You may have money tied up in other low return investments such as an endowment policy or other equity-based investment that you would like to move into property. Some people may have depreciating assets they now wish to sell in order to buy property.

Re-mortgaging Your Own Home

A very popular way to raise money initially is through releasing equity in the value of your home by re-mortgaging. You do not necessarily need to change lenders in order to release more equity from your own home but may be able to request a further advance. If you have not changed your mortgage deal for some time and have reverted to the lender's standard variable rate, you may be delighted to find that with a new deal you can increase your borrowing by enough for a deposit on a buy to let property without any noticeable increase in your monthly mortgage payments. We will be looking at mortgages in detail in the next chapter.

Personal Loans

Personal loans can offer relatively competitive rates of interest. Loans can carry strict redemption penalties, making it difficult to pay off some or all of the loan early. They may also have arrangement fees that you need to watch out for.

Credit Cards

When I learnt that it was possible to borrow money on credit cards at 0% finance for several months and then transfer the balance to another card before that period expires, resetting the 0% repayment clock and that this could be repeated indefinitely, I thought this was a great game!

I now have three cards that have allowed balance transfers to my bank account (though the rules of each change frequently). I acquired other cards and only found out afterwards that balance transfers to my account would not be allowed, only transfers between cards. Also, you are not told how much credit you will get until the application is complete, which is a little frustrating. I was given a credit limit of only £500 by one card provider which, it turned out, didn't allow transfer to my bank either.

For the amounts you are likely to be able to get, this seems to be a lot of work and requires discipline to keep on top of the game. If you don't have that discipline, you could be playing with fire. The application process can be slower than you might anticipate and the amount you will get is not normally known in advance.

Be aware also that, whilst 0% interest may be so, 'transfer fees' often apply to balance transfers so the money is not as free as you might think.

Check Your Credit Rating

If financial difficulties have led to a poor credit rating, it will be more difficult for you to borrow money by any of the above conventional means. You can and should check your own credit rating periodically, as you can be sure that lenders will do so. You can get reports of your own credit rating from www.checkmyfile.co.uk, which obtains information from all the main credit report agencies. You can also get reports direct from wwww.experian.co.uk and www.equifax.co.uk. If necessary, take steps to repair your credit rating. Further information about how to do so is available from these and other agencies.

Many people have problems at some stage with their credit rating; do not assume this prevents you from becoming a property investor. You may find a way round such difficulties by adopting any of the following strategies, which are also of value to those with more favourable credit scores.

The Many Forms of Leverage

Before we continue in our quest to raise finance, let's pause for a moment to consider some of the various forms that leverage can take. Millionaires are often masters at using leverage, in the form of other people's

- money

- experience

- ideas

- time

- work

The power of working with others through networking, teams and other means cannot be over-estimated. Bear this in mind when considering the following options for taking your investment activities to a higher level:

Joint Venture

Co-ownership of property may be a way forward for you. This could mean buying a property jointly with friends. Up to four named persons will normally be accepted for mortgage applications.

I have joint ventured with colleagues. In one case, the mortgage and property were solely in my name and my friend sent me a cheque for half the deposit sum plus expenses. I invited him to take a second charge on the property, but he declined, saying he thought it was not worth the extra hassle and expense. I agreed it was unnecessary, as I am so honest!

Taking Part in an Investment Club or Syndicate

You may wish to take part in a syndicate-type arrangement that will enable you to invest a smaller sum (often starting from as little as £1,000) on a more passive basis. Although £1,000 is a relatively small outlay in property, it is still a sizeable amount of cash so don't part with it lightly. Do undertake careful due diligence on who runs the scheme and what the proposed investments are before ever parting with cash.

Running an Investment Club or Syndicate

If you have sufficient contacts and a successful track record, you may wish to set up an investment club yourself, so that people can participate and benefit from deals that come your way. For general advice on setting up an investment club, see www.proshareclubs.co.uk. You will need to adapt your club for property and it's best to get a solicitor to help set up the terms and conditions.

Using Individual Investors

As above, with sufficient track record and contacts you may find individual investors who are willing to invest larger sums in your project/s. It can be more straightforward, of course, to deal with fewer and larger investors than many small ones.

Unlike joint ventures, where you would normally expect to split profits 50/50 (or in proportion to the amount put in), the expectation here is that the investor is more passive and the deal is normally structured accordingly. Investors would normally expect guaranteed returns, within a pre-agreed timeframe, of between 1% – 2% per month depending on the deal.

Bridging Finance

In the absence of private investors, or for the sake of speed where necessary, bridging finance can be used.

In the earlier chapter of Sourcing, Analysing and Structuring Below Market Value

Property Deals, we looked at using bridging to finance your BMV deal. Bridging finance can be used in place of the deposit, or as much as the whole purchase price, depending on circumstances. Bear in mind that some costs may well be involved upfront, even if ultimately you have created a 'no-money-down deal'.

For further information on how bridging finance can help, please visit www.aquickbridge.co.uk

Vendor Finance

Occasionally, it may be possible to get the seller or prospective buyer (where one is lined up to sell on to) to fund your deposit. This is fairly rare, although I do know people that have done this as well as some who have struck up a deal with a vendor to use a part of the vendor's released equity to fund future purchases in the short term, by paying them a set rate of interest monthly.

Gifted Deposits

If you are buying property off-plan, the developer may offer a gifted deposit. Beware, though, of artificial discounts with off-plan properties, which may have inflated prices that can lead to cashflow difficulties. I do not recommend buying newbuild properties and they have increasingly fallen out of favour with mortgage lenders too, particularly for buying to let.

The Leverage of Mortgage Borrowing

You might assume that if you invest in property which increases in value by 20% after one year then your money will increase by 20%. This would only apply, of course, if you bought the property for cash. However, using leverage you can multiply your capital appreciation.

Because you can borrow up to 85% of the purchase price to buy property, your seed money does not need to work too hard to grow. Just add leverage in the form of a buy to let mortgage.

Let's look at an example, to see how this works in practice:

- You manage to release £15,000 equity from your home, after increasing the value either through improvement or simply the benefit of time.

- With this £15,000 you buy an investment property for £100,000, using an 85% buy to let mortgage to finance the difference. (In practice, you will need to allow extra for expenses and so on; but let's keep it simple for now).

- After a year, the property has increased in value by 15% and it is now worth £115,000. So you now have an extra £15,000 value in the property. Your money has not grown by 15%, but by 100%.

- Consider that if you had bought shares with your £15,000 and they did as well as property, increasing by 15% over the year, your investment would now be worth £17,250. In that case, by not employing the use of leverage, your money would have grown by just £2,250 instead of £15,000.

The following chart illustrates the greater speed of growth that can be achieved by using leverage:

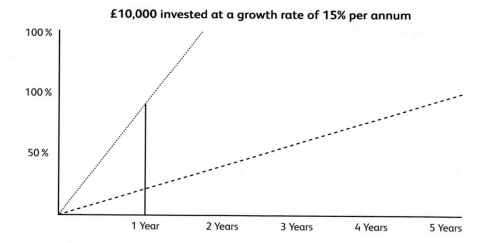

£10,000 invested at a growth rate of 15% per annum

The dotted line shows growth achieved using leverage, where an 85% mortgage is used to purchase a house at £100,000. The dashed line shows how growth will be slower and considerably less growth is achieved after one year without leverage (as would be the case if you bought property for cash). The solid vertical line emphasizes the huge and growing gap between the growth achievable with leverage as opposed to growth without. The trajectory of the dotted line showing the use of leverage is too steep to show - you may like to follow this yourself up to year five!

Whilst the power of leverage as demonstrated is great, things get better! The rate at which money can grow is further enhanced by the power of compound interest.

Compound Interest

> *"Compound interest is the eighth wonder of the world."*
> **Albert Einstein**

Compound interest occurs when you invest money and you earn interest on your capital, then the next year you earn interest on both your original capital and the interest from the first year. In the third year you earn interest on your capital and the first two years' interest.

The concept of earning interest on your interest is the miracle of compounding.

You may believe that if your money grows by say 10% a year, then after 10 years it will have grown by 100%. But this is not so. In reality, the money increases by more each year due to the effects of compounding.

You can see how this works, by getting your calculator out and working through an example.

For the sake of example, let's say you have £100,000 that, by investing in property, grows by 15% per annum. You can see how much this increases each year by doing the following exercise on your calculator:

- 1.15 (representing 15% growth) X (press the multiply key, on some calculators twice) £100,000 = £115,000

- After one year your money has increased by a straightforward £15,000

- Now SIMPLY PRESS THE EQUALS KEY ON THE CALCULATOR AGAIN FOR EACH SUCCESSIVE YEAR:

- So, by pressing = a second time, you will see that your capital is now worth £132,250.

- This is not merely another £15,000 but is COMPOUNDED: It is a 15% increase not on the original £100,000, but on the amount of £115,000 that existed at the end of year one.

- Again, for a third time = £152,087.50

- And at the end of the fourth year, your money is worth £174,900.20

- After five years, your money is worth £201,135.71

- Your money has **doubled** in five years, with the help of compounding interest. If £15,000 alone were added each year, this would have amounted to £175,000, but the cumulative effect of compounding increases this amount by more than another £26,000.

The Rule of 72

There is a handy shortcut to help you work out the effects of compound interest, known as the Rule of 72. It states that you can find out how many years it will take for your investment to double by dividing 72 by the percentage rate of growth. So it will take 9 years for your investment to double if it grows at 8% a year (72/8=9). But it will only take 6 years to double if your investment grows at 12% and so on. The Rule of 72 only provides an approximate answer but it is a handy quick guide.

To give another example, if you receive 10% interest on your savings, your money will double in 7.2 years. If your property is appreciating in value by 5% per year, it will take 14.4 years to double your money. If it appreciates by 20% per year, then it will take 3.6 years to double in value. The Rule of 72 is simply dividing the number 72 by the interest or the percentage of gain in value to give the relative speed at which your money will double.

Gearing

Another important aspect to investing is gearing. I'll give you an example that demonstrates the part gearing plays in investments:

- Three people have £100,000 each:

    o Jim inherits his money and knows nothing about investing

    o Sophie is a young professional who knows a thing or two

    o You have read Property Investing Success, and are now a sophisticated investor!

Let's assume for this example that property increases by an average of 5% a year:

- Jim wants to find a home for his windfall and has heard that property is a good investment. He buys one property for £100,000 cash. After ten years, it is worth £162,889 (which is 5% per annum compound growth). He has made £62,889 profit on his initial investment, or **63%**.

- Sophie understands the value of leverage but decides to tread cautiously. She buys two properties for £100,000 each by using 50% mortgages along with £50,000 cash for each property. At the end of ten years these two properties, which cost a total of £200,000, are worth £325,778, an increase of £125,778. Sophie's profit is **126%**, or double that of Jim's.

- You understand the power of leverage and of compounding and decide to go into top gear! You go for 85% mortgages, gearing up your purchases to the maximum, to put together with your £100,000 and buy properties with a total value of £666,666 with 15% deposits on each. At the end of 10 years, your properties are worth £1,085,928. You have made £419,262. That is a **420%** increase on your initial investment.

- It is possible that you not only left your properties with the **equity** increasing for ten years, but also continued to release further equity from the properties as they increased in value and were able to buy even more properties. This would cause the initial investment to multiply even quicker.

This is the magic of buy to let: the combination of compound interest, leverage and gearing. Well done you!

So, what are **you** going to be doing for the next ten years?

Financing Your Portfolio From Within

Assuming in time your first investment property has scope for more borrowing, many buy to let lenders will allow you to release (or draw down) further equity just six months after the date of purchase. Some do not even have a minimum time before you can draw down; you will need to check this with your lender.

The amount of extra borrowing will bring the new total mortgage to the maximum borrowing allowed (such as 85%) of the NEW property value. A surveyor of the lender's choice will visit the property to assess the current value.

This should be a fairly straightforward procedure, not involving solicitors. This is not the same as a re-mortgage and the extra borrowing may, depending on the lender, follow the terms of the original mortgage deal and will not incur any penalties.

You will appreciate that, just as the use of leverage for the initial property purchase enables a faster level of growth, so this rapid pace of growth now becomes self-perpetuating. Hence, if property prices were increasing by 15% per annum and you bought a very cheap place with £15,000 cash, the property value will have increased by £2,250 after one year, (too insignificant to be of much use). However, having used the leverage of an 85% mortgage to buy somewhere for £100,000 that increased by £15,000, you could now release further equity to buy property number two. At this rate, you can buy two further properties by year three, whereas the cash buyer would still have inadequate funds for property number two.

When you have several properties, you needn't wait until the value of one increases by enough for your next deposit. The minimum extra borrowing per property is often just £5,000, so if you require £20,000 you can draw just £5,000 from four properties if necessary. Of course, there will be some administration costs each time, so this needs to be taken into account. This is the principle on which we achieved the expansion of our portfolio in our early years of investing.

If you buy below market value of course, as I do now, the portfolio can be refinanced and grown even quicker.

How Much Money Can You Borrow for Buy to Let?

Many people do not realise that the greatest thing about buy to let borrowing is that it is not limited or dependent upon your own earnings, unlike a mortgage for your own home. There is no real ceiling to the amount of borrowing you can have for buy to let properties. As long as the figures stack up to make the investment viable and you continue to meet your lender's requirements (including paying the mortgage), there is no effective limit to the amount of borrowing you can have.

Whilst individual lenders normally have a maximum for the borrowing allowed, you are not, of course, limited to one lender.

Although lenders differ as to the exact parameters of borrowing, they may require the expected rental income to be equivalent to around 125% of the monthly mortgage payments. You need to be able to play around with the figures, to know what your maximum borrowing for a given property will be. Your mortgage broker will be able to advise you.

Number Crunching

In this section, I will show you all the figure work you need to decide the viability of a given property investment.

When considering a particular investment property to buy, you need to know the expected rental income that it will produce as this is important, both in terms of the property's yield and how much you will be able to borrow for the property.

For the purposes of these examples, it is assumed you will be getting an interest-only mortgage. The pros and cons of an interest-only versus interest and capital mortgage will be discussed further in the next chapter, but for now we make this assumption as most investors do opt for interest-only mortgages on investment properties.

As the lender in this example requires the monthly rent to be a minimum of 130% of the monthly mortgage payments, it can be expressed as:

- Monthly mortgage payments X 130% = minimum rent allowed

If you know the rent will be £700 per calendar month and that the lender requires the rent to be 130% of the monthly mortgage payments, you can work out the maximum monthly mortgage payments as:

- £700 / 1.3 = £538.46 (this is the maximum monthly mortgage payment)

Now that you have worked out the maximum monthly mortgage payment allowed given the rent achievable, you can calculate the maximum loan for the property (providing this does not exceed the maximum 85% of the property price, or value). You will need to know the lender's standard variable rate of interest or the rate the lender will use for this calculation. In this case, I am assuming an interest rate of 5%:

- £538.46 x 12 / 0.05 = £129,230.40 (the maximum loan*)

* Given that this amount does not breach the 85% maximum borrowing or other maximum, according to the lender.

The above calculations demonstrate each step but can be further summarised in practice, starting from knowing the rent to calculating the maximum borrowing you can get:

- £700 x 12 / 1.30 / 0.05 = £129,230.40

(pennies being rounded down in the above equations)

From this maximum loan, you can decide the maximum property value you can consider, given that the rent is £700 pcm and the SVR is 5%. If you do not wish to leave any money in the deal, your maximum buy price may be no more than the £129,230.40 (possibly less costs) shown above. If, however, you are happy to leave a 15% deposit in the property, your maximum buy price may be:

- £129,230.40/85% = £152,035.76

At a later stage, you may know the amount of the loan you are getting and want to remind yourself or work out what your monthly mortgage payments will be at a given rate of interest, which is very useful, for example, when a rate change is expected or imminent. This may be done in the following way:

- (Loan amount X interest rate) / 12 = monthly mortgage payments

So, given the above figures, if the interest rate went up to 6% your monthly payments would be:

- (£129,230.40 x 0.06) / 12 = £646.15

Clearly, a climate of low interest rates has a positive impact. While interest rates are relatively low, you can borrow more than when they are higher. This not only makes your first property more affordable, but also allows you to expand your portfolio more quickly.

The Gross Yield

To ascertain the gross yield for the property use the following simple formula. It is very useful for comparing the attractiveness of different options: which property will give me a better yield, property A or property B? You should familiarise yourself with this formula, which can be looked at from a number of angles, depending on which factors are known:

- yield = (rent x 12) / price x 100

- rent = (yield x price) / 12 /100

- price = (rent x 12) / yield x 100

The main usefulness of the gross yield is:

1. For comparing the attractiveness of properties.

2. To act as a quick and easy guide to whether the figures will stack up for the property; that is whether, given the rent achievable and the price, it is likely to be a feasible buy.

Normally, you should not accept any yield below 5% and ideally it should be higher. To ensure good cashflow, the yield should always be more than the interest rate being paid on the mortgage. Other factors may occasionally over-ride this rule, especially if the property is suitable for improvement or if you are confident of rapid capital appreciation and being able to draw equity out or sell before long. I would definitely NOT recommend this as a general strategy. I know investors who have done so and then the market has turned round quite suddenly and bitten them, leaving some badly hurt and others completely wiped out! Do not be one of those who gets caught out in this way.

Stay away from 'over-trading' and cashflow problems at all times. Cashflow is King!

How Important is Cashflow?

Turnover is Vanity, Profit is Sanity but Cashflow is King!

I have already talked about the power of leverage and compound interest working together with capital appreciation to increase your wealth; BUT remember that as long as the equity remains in the properties it is not in your hands. You cannot use it to buy food for the family.

One of the great benefits of buy to let is that your properties can supply you with income as well as capital appreciation, so there is no need to sell in order to have money to live on.

This **cash flow** is of the **utmost importance** to the **success and sustainability** of your business. Ignore it at your peril.

You might decide to withdraw equity from the properties and spend it, but don't overdo it. Be careful not to upset the positive cashflow of the portfolio!

"Buying properties enables you to effectively grow your own money tree with many branches. The income may not be vast from one property but should eventually be sufficient to replace your previous main income source. Your properties will keep you busy enough," says Dave.

> ## Excerpt from Dave's Diary...
>
>
> **Thursday 4th March, 2004:**
> I received a bill for the double glazing at 17H, but I'm not going to pay it yet because one of the windows is cracked, one of the vents is on the wrong way round and the mastic on the outside of the bathroom window is not in yet, because the overflow is leaking and the outside is wet and the mastic won't stick while it's wet. I phoned them up and said I'm not going to pay and they said "alright then"; they were quite happy with that.

"However, I suggest you are cautious and realistic about the net income you receive from your properties before making any life-changing decisions. You need to allow for fluctuations in the income due, for example, to interest rate increases or property voids."

The Importance of Net Yield

The usual figure used to consider permissible borrowing for a new property deal is the gross yield, as discussed above. However, it is important that you understand the difference between the gross yield and the actual net income you will receive from your property. The consideration of expenses is a must, as the battle to keep expenses down is key to success in buy to let.

Net yield can be worked out in a number of ways according to preference, or your particular aims at the time. There is no standard method or terminology for how to work out the net yield (other than the Inland Revenue's determination of this) and various commentators may refer to:

- Net yield

- Return on Investment (ROI)

- Internal Rate of Return (IRR)

- Return on Equity (ROE)

- Cash on Cash Return

These are simply variations on the same theme of ways to consider the returns on your investment, each choosing a slightly different angle of looking at the figures. You will find a way that you feel most comfortable with in due course.

Here is how I worked out our net income:

- Ratio of expenses to income = (expenses/rent) x 100%

As an example, I worked out our figures for data relating to a particular tax year. This included 27 properties, 10 of which were purchased during the year (as well as one being sold, entailing a fairly long void).

The average expenses including the mortgages were 74.67% of rent and so the net profit was 25.33% of incoming rent.

If I excluded mortgages from the figures just to get a different perspective on the expenses, the average expenses per property were 19.18% of rent. This figure ranged from 2.75% (a house which was occupied throughout the year) to 47.2% (a flat that was bought in October that year, needed work and suffered a void). The average expenses for houses was 16.52% and for flats was 22.96%

Bear in mind that if you pay for a full management service, you will pay 15%+ in expenses on that alone. It is not surprising that the average expenses for flats were more, since they entail compulsory block maintenance costs (normally known as the service charge).

The average percentage spent on expenses was less the following year, as we had a much lower percentage of newly purchased properties.

The above analysis does not take into account the general expenses incurred by the business which amounted to a further 3%-5% of total expenses per property.

Don't forget, when calculating expenses against income for tax purposes, that 10% wear and tear allowance can be claimed on furnished properties.

The above expenses do include costs involved when a property is first bought. As we often buy scruffy properties, this can be a fairly significant percentage of overall profit for the property's first year (when new carpets and some refurbishment are likely to be required) and a void is inevitable at that stage.

The analysis above demonstrates how you should exercise control over your expenses. Keep accurate records of expenses so that you can quantify your net profit and consider how it can be improved on a continual basis, as well as for tax purposes.

I find that a big problem for many property investors is that they like all the 'sexy' bits about the business but fail to focus on what I call the housework: the ongoing concerns and cares connected to any business.

Let's face it, keeping an eye on your expenses is about as interesting as watching magnolia paint dry on yet another wall. Some investors fail ultimately because they don't face the boring but important aspects to the business and so they practically die of boredom; or at least, their business does! Or else they decide to spice up their life by going and doing something else sexy like investing abroad where they know less than enough.

Don't be a fool. Stay focused and committed. This is not sexy - it's survival! You'll be far sexier when you get rich, trust me:-) You just need to stay on track to get there!

Tax for Property Investors

The tax treatment of buy to let investors is very different from that of people who buy property with the primary aim of selling for profit. Regardless of whether you buy as a limited company or as an individual, a couple, a group or a partnership, these taxes will apply. You must be familiar with what the tax requirements are.

Key taxes for property investors include:

- Income Tax

- Capital Gains Tax

- Inheritance Tax

- Stamp Duty

Taxation levels are decided and may be changed annually with the Chancellor's budget.

Property investing offers various concessions to reduce your tax burden. You must be aware of these in order to take advantage of them and this section will help. Your accountant should advise in detail with regard to your individual circumstances.

While net rental income is subject to income tax, many of the expenses you incur in the business of property investing are tax deductible, including the interest on mortgage payments. This includes the whole of the payments for an interest only mortgage, but does not include the capital portion of a capital and interest payment mortgage.

Although the costs involved in the purchase of property will not be taken into account for tax purposes while the property ownership is ongoing, they **will** be considered allowable expenses against the capital gain when the property is sold (along with the costs of sale).

Buying to let is considered an investment business, whereas buying property to sell primarily for profit is considered a trading business: you trade in property. As a property trading business, you will be required to register for VAT if you exceed the annual threshold of £60,000 on profits from property sales.

For more details about VAT registration, see ww.hmce.gov.uk.

Should I have a Limited Company?

It must be emphasised that your accountant should help you to decide what's right for you as many individual factors need to be considered, including your long-term strategy and exit plans. I am not an expert on tax matters, which can be very complex especially with regard to limited companies. You must seek expert guidance from your accountant or other tax advisor.

In general terms, there are two schools of thought about whether investors should operate as a limited company:

- Many argue that it is not worth considering the extra hassle of buying property as a limited company (it can be more difficult to find a lender as a limited company, particularly if you are also a new investor). Note that if you buy property in your own name and later wish to change the ownership to your limited company, you would have to sell the property to the company which would then be required to pay stamp duty again. With double tax as well as buying and selling expenses, this would probably prove to be financially unviable. So you need to be sure how you want to own the property at the outset.

- The argument in favour of having a limited company is that you can use the company structure as a tax shield, and ring-fence some of your wealth. Recognise however that the limited liability you might expect to be associated with a limited company is not likely to apply, as you will almost certainly be required to give a personal guarantee for the mortgage money. Some investors use a limited company to **manage** their properties for financial or tax advantage reasons. Others buy to let as individuals but buy to sell, where different rules apply, as a company.

For many investors, it is not imperative to buy property in the name of a limited company and, generally, it is more straightforward not to; for example when applying for a mortgage. However, if you decide that the tax advantages outweigh the drawbacks for you, or have serious ambitions to expand your empire aggressively, take on investors and, possibly, one day become a publicly listed company, you will want to set up a limited company to buy all your properties from the outset.

The decision whether to set up a limited company is far from straightforward and can even make accountants flinch. When I approached my accountant for advice about whether to set up a limited company to buy some properties, he said there was, in fact, no definitive answer to the question of whether this would be the best option financially in the long run. It would depend on:

- Any future changes in government regulations regarding tax and other laws for limited companies

- How my circumstances changed and developed over time - neither of which can be fully predicted

I decided to hedge my bets by setting up a limited company with which I bought six properties.

Whether you buy properties in the name of a limited company or not, you can use your limited company to effect tax advantages by using the company to manage the properties.

Corporation Tax is payable on a company's total profits and capital gains and this has different bands and rates than for an individual, as shown in the table below.

Corporation Tax Rates for a Small Company, on Total Profits and Gains:

Corporation tax on profits - £ per year (unless stated)

Profits	Rate applied	Rate payable on profits earned from 1 April 2008
Up to £300,000	Small companies' rate	21 per cent
£300,001 - £1,500,000	Marginal relief from main rate	Between 21 per cent and 28 per cent
£1,500,000+	Main rate	28 per cent

Tax for limited companies is dealt with differently than for individuals. The sale of property owned by a limited company is not eligible per se for capital gains tax.

It should also be noted that a company does not have the benefit of any annual personal allowance for Income Tax or Capital Gains Tax (CGT) purposes. For property owned privately by individuals, the first £9,600 of profit on sale per person will be exempt from Capital Gains Tax for the tax year 2008/2009, providing that the property was bought to let. CGT (or its reliefs) will not apply to property that is specifically bought to sell for profit; buying to sell is considered 'trading' rather than 'investing' and profits are consequently treated as income rather than a capital gain.

In summary, the decision whether to buy property as a limited company is far from straightforward. However, there is a useful business saying "you should not allow the tax tail to wag the financial dog." In other words, wider commercial drivers should be the main consideration in our decision-making process, rather than tax alone which will follow behind one way or another!

While it is difficult to predict long term, at the level of an individual deal and on a short-term basis, current taxation policies may have a greater predictability and, therefore, more direct influence on how a deal should be structured.

Income Tax

Income Tax is only due on taxable income that is above your tax-free allowances, for individuals. For the year 2008-2009, the basic personal allowance, or tax-free amount (for those aged under 65) is £5,435.

Income Tax rates above this allowance vary by tax band and by type of income.

The Income Tax bands for 2008-2009 are:

- starting rate band - up to £2,320

- basic rate band - £2,320 to £36,000

- higher rate band - from £36,001

For the tax year 2008-2009 the Income Tax due, after tax-free allowances, on earned and rental income is:

- 10% where the income falls within the starting rate band

- 20% where it falls above the starting rate band but within the basic rate band

- 40% where it falls in the higher rate band

On dividend income (from shares in UK companies) you pay:

- 10% if it falls within the basic rate tax band

- 32.5% if it falls within the higher rate tax band

Capital Gains Tax

For individuals, profit arising from the sale of property that has been bought to let out is considered a capital gain for tax purposes. A capital gain is, essentially, the difference between the purchase price and the price at which you sell the property, less allowable deductions of expenses including:

- All purchase and sale costs for the property will be deductible against CGT; further allowances, reliefs and exemptions may apply, particularly if the property has, at some stage, been your principal primary residence.

- For the year 2008 – 2009, CGT is charged at the single rate of 18%.

- There is an annual exempt (tax-free) capital gains allowance for each individual and in the tax year 2008 – 2009 this is £9,600.

The treatment of profits upon sale as a capital gain is generally an advantage that the buy to let investor has over those who buy to sell. The latter, being considered to trade property for profit are considered to have generated income by selling. In this case, all profits will be treated as income for tax purposes.

For more information about the tax implications of renting out a property, visit the Inland Revenue online at www.inlandrevenue.gov.uk or contact your local tax office and request a copy of the Inland Revenue booklet IR150, Taxation of Rents: A Guide to Property Income and request further details about capital gains tax.

Stamp Duty

This is an indirect tax on property ownership, paid to the Inland Revenue at the time a property is purchased, for properties costing over £125,000 and according to the following price bands:

Property up to £125,000	no stamp duty
Property between £125,000 - £250,000	stamp duty at 1 per cent
Property between £250,001 - £500,000	stamp duty at 3 per cent
Property priced £500,001 +	stamp duty at 4 per cent

Your Will and Use of Trusts

As part of your longer term tax planning strategy, you should arrange to have a Last Will and Testament drawn up to safeguard your family's interests after your death, which ideally should be done through a solicitor. If your net wealth is (or is likely to be) over £312,000, the threshold for Inheritance Tax (which along with all taxes is reviewed each year) it becomes even more imperative that you plan your estate effectively. Many people will fall into this tax net simply on the basis of the value in their own home, particularly those living in London and the south-east.

One of the first things your solicitor should advise is that a husband and wife own properties as 'tenants in common in equal shares', rather than as 'joint tenants' (which can be changed retrospectively). Then in turn, each partner should leave the first £312,000 of their net worth in their Will to their children, in a discretionary trust with the partner. This can potentially save the children over £100,000 in inheritance tax.

By setting up such a discretionary trust, the children will have no legal right to claim possession of the property or properties before the death of the second partner, but will simply be protected from the apportioned Inheritance Tax that would otherwise be due. When the second partner dies, the children will not then be liable for Inheritance Tax on the first £312,000. If this arrangement did not exist, the second partner would inherit all the wealth of the first partner by default (being next of kin); then, on their death, the children would be saddled with a much higher tax bill.

It is advisable to use a probate solicitor for advice and help in these matters. Your accountant may be able to recommend a solicitor, or you can find one independently or, better still, by recommendation.

Other important areas to consider in conjunction with lifetime financial planning are life-assurance and pension planning. You may wish to discuss these with your probate solicitor or accountant too.

With all the areas covered in this section, there is potential for overlap of advice from your accountant and probate solicitor. It is up to you how you play your cards, or which exact advice you take, but either way it is important to remember that the responsibility is ultimately your own.

One matter you may like to discuss with your accountant or probate solicitor, if you have children, is setting up a Trust to buy property for the children. I did this for my three children and now act as trustee for three houses which I hold in an Accumulation and Maintenance Trust for the three children. This requires a separate bank account and tax returns and different tax rates apply.

When the children are 25 they will have full entitlement to the properties and profits held in trust for them, or we could grant them entitlement earlier at our discretion. I am entitled to use profits in the Trust for the children's welfare and education in the meantime (thankfully, as my daughter is off to university soon!)

Note that children cannot own property in their own name before the age of 18.

As your business grows, you need to manage growth by planning in accordance with your long-term goals and ultimately your exit strategy from the business. Get your Last Will and Testament written up and be prepared to revise it as time goes by. If you have children, consider a Trust for them.

In this chapter we have looked in some detail at the potential benefits of using leverage in the form of mortgage borrowing for buy to let investments. We then went on to consider the tax elements to organising your financial affairs. The next chapter looks in depth at choosing the right mortgage for you.

Chapter 5

Choose Your Mortgage and Insurance

"Give me a lever long enough and a prop strong enough, and I can single-handedly move the world."
Archimedes

It is important that you find the right mortgage if you plan to use one, as is normally advisable for investors, before setting out to buy your investment property.

For each individual, the various features of mortgages must be weighed up according to your own circumstances and long-term goals, as well as your preferences, attitude to risk and assessment of likely future interest rate movements and market conditions. I recommend you use a variety of sources, especially in the early stages of your search. When I started out, I found a good starting point was to read mortgage magazines, which give good general advice, some also have websites such as www.mortgageadvisormag.co.uk and www.whatmortgageonline.co.uk.

Buy to let mortgages have only been available since 1996 and were originally devised by the Association of Residential Letting Agents (ARLA) working with a handful of mortgage lenders including Nat West, Birmingham Midshires, Paragon Mortgages and Clydesdale Bank. It was with the introduction of the Assured Shorthold Tenancy Agreement (Short Assured Tenancy in Scotland) and relatively recent changes in the housing law, that ARLA was able to put forward a case of reassurance to lenders about the security of their loan.

When choosing a mortgage, it is important to consider not only the current mortgage being sought but what scope the lender provides for further mortgages or advances, as this will have a crucial impact on your future ability to grow your business.

It is worth noting that lenders differ in the way their business is structured internally: they may be a bank, a building society, or simply a mortgage lending company. This could have an impact on you. Ask the lender or your IFA for further details of this.

Remember that buy to let mortgages have only been around since 1996 and the property market has, until recently, been very positive since. We should not take for granted the opportunity to leverage money which these mortgages provide.

The credit crunch of 2008 has seen lenders tightening their lending criteria and raising interest rates in line with LIBOR, making it more difficult for borrowers. Some experts predict that the credit crunch will continue and get even worse over the next two or more years. An excellent credit rating will become increasingly important to borrowers seeking to be looked upon favourably.

On the plus side, future growth of the private rental market is predicted to continue.

Using a Mortgage Broker

I suggest that after having carried out your own initial research into lenders and deals currently available, you consult a few mortgage brokers or, as they are otherwise known, independent financial advisors (IFAs). I introduced this important subject in Planning and Risk Assessment. To recap:

It is normally a good idea to use a broker when choosing a mortgage, for several reasons: they have the resources to quickly scan all lenders and rates available, which are continually being updated; they often have access to favourable rates and deals with lenders that are not available to direct applicants; they can also help to fill in the application form and offer advice as to the verification documents that different lenders will require to see.

There are many choices for finding an independent financial advisor or mortgage advisor. Working with a broker who is familiar with buy to let and creative finance solutions can be invaluable.

Mortgage brokers can have varying levels of independence and scope in the products they offer and it is important to establish this from the outset. Ask each broker if they have access to all, or at least most, buy to let mortgages currently available and also whether they are tied to an insurance company or other body. I have used a broker who is connected with an insurance company, but is happy for me to sign papers declining any insurance offered.

Mention to your broker any lenders you have come across yourself, as well as making clear all the mortgage features you are looking for. Unless you make clear all the features of a mortgage that are important to you, brokers may tend to assume that you will simply be interested in the lowest headline rate (a term given to the current special deal rates on offer), especially if they feel you are going round asking for several rate quotes. Whilst it is generally good to keep expenses down in business, I believe that choosing the right mortgage and the right lender is so important to your future success that it is essential you consider the wider merits of any lenders under consideration. You need to convey to your broker that you are looking for a quality lender, not just the headline rate!

As with other professionals who will be an important part of your business team, it is important to establish a good and trusting relationship with your broker.

Having an IFA can also be a strategic advantage when you put forward an offer on a property if you are buying through an estate agent, as the agent will often want to verify that you are in a position to proceed with the mortgage required before accepting your offer. If you go directly to a lender, it is most probable the lender will refuse to talk to estate agents or other third parties, so your ability to proceed cannot be verified. Your broker, with your permission, will be happy to confirm that you have a lender's agreement in principle (AIP) for your required finance.

If you are buying property below market value, and particularly if there are complications involved such as a rent-back or instant re-mortgage required, it is imperative that you choose a broker who is familiar with these issues and knows how to present information positively to the lender. Professional brokerage companies work with packagers whose role it is to present your application appropriately to the lender; and whilst you will have no direct contact with the packager, this is an essential role that should not be overlooked and to which a smaller or independent broker may not have access.

Interest Rates

The cost of mortgage borrowing is traditionally dependent on the base rate of interest set for borrowing by the Bank of England (BoE), although the current credit crunch in 2008 has seen mortgage rates increasingly dependent on Libor, which stands for London Interbank Offered Rate.

It is worth understanding a little about the money markets, especially in today's financial climate, and how this affects us as borrowers. Libor is the main setter of interest rates in the London wholesale money market. Unlike the bank rate, which is set directly by the Bank of England, Libor rates are set by the demand and supply of money as banks lend to each other (or not, as the case may be).

Libor is used to price all kinds of financial instruments such as loans and mortgages. Instruments in several other currencies are also priced relative to Libor, such is the size of the London market.

The three-month Libor rate normally trades at a small premium of around 0.15% above where the market thinks the bank rate will be in three months' time but, in recent months, the Libor rate has shot up to 6.6% and has stayed around that level, recently hitting an eight-and-a-half year high of 6.7%. This reflected a reluctance by banks to lend to each other for fear that the counterparty may have problems and not be able to pay back the money; all being related to the US sub-prime mortgage crisis.

The BoE's monetary policy committee (MPC) holds monthly meetings to decide whether to raise or lower the interest rate, taking into account various economic factors and seeking to maximise or maintain healthy economic conditions for the country as a whole, in line with government expectations. One of the government's aims is to seek economic stability for the country and low inflation. However, the urgency of the banking crisis in October 2008 has seen the government take over control of the decision to cut interest rates by 0.5% with further cuts expected.

It is increasingly important to watch and understand the Libor rate, as mortgage lenders align with this. A lender's standard variable rate (SVR) is traditionally between 1%-2% higher than the Bank of England base rate or, more commonly now, above Libor. The SRV is charged when customers are not within the terms of a 'special deal'. Each lender's SVR will also vary and this should be taken into account when choosing a lender; a 1% discount rate by one lender may be equivalent only to the SVR of another lender.

In practice, mortgage deals are often offered initially at a fixed, discount, flexible or tracker rate, often for the first two to five years. You need to consider carefully and understand the relative merits of each before choosing. Don't forget also to take into account that deals vary in the redemption penalty period (RPP) that can accompany them, ranging from none to a few years beyond the special rate deal during which time you will revert to the lender's standard variable rate (or pay a penalty to exit).

Exit penalties themselves also vary, normally equivalent to between three and six months' mortgage payments.

Fixed Rate Mortgages

Many landlords opt for fixed rate deals, which offer peace of mind about rate changes. It should be noted that the rates for fixed deals are set by industry experts taking into account future predicted rate movements; hence when rates are predicted to rise, fixed rates are often set higher than the standard variable rate. The redemption penalty period may also be longer at such times.

Fixed deals may range from less than a year (often these do not offer such good value as it appears, giving a very low initial rate for only a short period, sometimes with penalty periods that overhang), to the whole mortgage term. I would not personally consider a full mortgage term fix - a lot can happen in 30 years!

Discount Mortgages

Discount mortgages can work out cheaper than fixed rate deals but, of course, you need to accept that rates can go up as well as down. You have no protection against a rise in your mortgage repayments.

Other variations may also be available, such as capped or stepped discounts.

Flexible Mortgages

Some landlords like to choose a flexible mortgage as you can overpay or underpay. This can help alleviate potential cash flow problems: you can overpay when things are going well then, during periods of void or tenant rent payment troubles, you can underpay without penalties being incurred. You can usually take a payment break too.

Rates for flexible mortgages may be slightly higher then ordinary discount mortgages, making the monthly payments higher. Interest is often calculated daily for flexible mortgages, which can be an added bonus when you are in relative credit. A positive advantage can be gained in both the short and long-term, when interest is calculated daily, especially when rates are heading downward.

Whether or not you have a 'flexible mortgage' by name, it may be that there is some allowance for making overpayments to your mortgage. If this is a feature you would like, ask the question when arranging your mortgage.

Tracker Mortgages

Whilst all lenders generally raise or lower their interest rates in keeping with changes in the Bank of England base rate, they may do so in such a way as to maintain their own advantage above the borrowers. For example, when the base rate goes up, lenders are quick to raise their own rate also, but when the base rate goes down they can act more slowly and may not mirror the exact amount. With a tracker mortgage the lender commits to move rates faithfully, as per terms agreed in the mortgage conditions.

Many mortgages track the Bank of England base rate, but some track LIBOR. Most LIBOR mortgages track three-month LIBOR: they have a three-monthly rate review. Although these are variable-rate deals, they are not subject to change as often as those based on a lender's Standard Variable Rate (SVR) or the Bank of England base rate.

Switching or Re-mortgaging to a Better Deal

When your mortgage comes out of the special rate and/or redemption penalty period, you can normally switch to a new deal with the same lender, or you may re-mortgage to a different lender. Switching to a better deal at that stage can save you hundreds of pounds a year in interest. You will, of course, need to weigh up all the expenses involved.

It may be that the best rate can be achieved by switching lenders, but this will involve more time, hassle and paperwork. It will also require you to employ the services of a solicitor, unlike switching to a new deal. You may be happy with your current lender but simply wish to take advantage of a new deal that switches you to a lower, or fixed, rate of interest.

I have always put a note on my calendar of the date on which I can switch deals for each mortgage. With some lenders you can apply for a new deal up to three months before expiry of the previous one, which can help you avoid having the mortgage revert to standard variable rates in the interim! Also, if you think interest rates are set to rise it is a good idea to fix a rate as early as you can.

You do need to watch out these days for the charges involved, even simply in a new deal. Lenders' charges have increased dramatically over the last year and it can now sometimes mean that, on balance, it's cheaper to stay on the standard variable rate for now! Make sure when you calculate the cost of the deal over the whole period versus staying on the SVR, you include all costs!

Interest Only or Capital and Interest Mortgage?

You will need to decide whether you want an interest only mortgage or to pay capital and interest. This must be decided at the outset and you will need to check whether these options are offered. Some lenders allow for part interest only and part capital repayment loans.

It should be noted that only the interest portion of mortgage payments is deductible as an expense against tax. A capital and interest mortgage will have higher monthly payments and may therefore require lower levels of borrowing to achieve the lender's requirements. Such a mortgage may suit those who are more risk averse and less interested in growing their portfolio.

Where an interest only mortgage is offered, enquire whether the borrower is required to have a capital repayment vehicle in place and/or life assurance. Lenders are often vague about this, as they do not wish to appear irresponsible by suggesting it is fine not to have any repayment vehicle. It is worth asking if any such vehicle or insurance will need to be assigned to the lender as a condition of the mortgage; if the answer is "no" that means it is not compulsory.

You may decide it is a good idea to have either a capital and interest mortgage or to have a capital repayment vehicle in place (this would be, for example, an endowment/pension/ISA/life insurance policy). This must be weighed up against the affordability of running the mortgage, as all these things increase the monthly costs. Again, only the interest portion of a mortgage payment is deductible as an expense against tax, not the capital portion (if paid).

Many investors who are serious about growing their portfolios at maximum pace opt for an interest only mortgage with no repayment vehicle. In this case, your exit plan may be to sell some properties at retirement to pay off the mortgages in full; on others you may decide to keep for life.

Mortgage Term: How Long Can the Mortgage Be?

It can be advantageous to maximise the mortgage term or length, as this offers scope for the property to gain most capital value during the term. It should be noted that with an interest only mortgage the payments do not vary according to the length of the mortgage, but only with the interest rate since only interest is being repaid. However, with a capital and interest mortgage, the monthly mortgage payments will vary with the mortgage term (the shorter the term, the higher the monthly payments) as the capital portion must be repaid at different rates according to the total period available for this. See the Mortgage Cost Calculator.

Whilst maximising the mortgage length allows more time for capital appreciation, it should not be overlooked that the mortgage will work out more expensive in the long term as more payments are made. With a capital repayment mortgage, the monthly repayments for too short a term may prove simply unaffordable on an investment property with a fair to high level of gearing.

The lender may stipulate, in any case, a minimum loan duration of five years and maximum loan duration of thirty years. Other limiting factors may also apply, for example that the loan must terminate by the borrower's age of retirement. However, lenders' rules vary and may be subject to change so do ask at the time of applying for a mortgage.

In the case of leasehold property, the length of the lease can dictate limitations to the mortgage term. The lender may require forty years to be remaining on the lease length by the end of the mortgage term, so if the lease length at the time of purchase is only sixty years, the maximum loan term available will be twenty years. If you arrange for the lease to be lengthened during the period of ownership, you will be able to change the mortgage term.

Leverage - It's What Mortgages Are All About

Shrewd investors will often use mortgages to buy investment properties even if they could pay cash. By maximising your leverage through using mortgages, you can maximise your capital gains. This has been discussed at more length in the previous chapter Money Matters.

What loan-to-value (LTV) ratio of borrowing does the lender offer? This is the percentage you can borrow relative to the value of the property. The final decision of value lies with the lender's valuation officer, rather than the price you have agreed to pay.

Many lenders now offer 85% LTV, although some lenders offer less and this may vary according to the borrower's status. Remember, the higher the percentage of borrowing, the greater your leverage. Working out how much you will be able to borrow for any given property deal was examined in detail in the Money Matters chapter. The overall percentage of leverage, or borrowing, which you employ either for a single investment property or a portfolio, is also often referred to as your 'gearing'.

In close connection with the consideration of LTV is the lender's requirement for the rent to be a certain percentage above the monthly mortgage payments (usually at the lender's standard variable rate, regardless of any special deal rates). The rent may be required to be 130% of the monthly mortgage payments, for example. Some lenders offer a more relaxed 125% and some as little as 100%, although you must appreciate that, while this enables you to borrow more, there is no inbuilt allowance for any voids or hiccups which is more perilous to cashflow and, for the same reason, 130% is safer.

The lender will assess the rent achievable either through their surveyor at the time of the valuation report, or by asking a local letting agent (which may be of their own choice, or by letter obtained at your request to the lender). The agent may be required to be a member of ARLA (Association of Residential Letting Agents) for the lender's satisfaction.

What Sort of Borrower Are You?

A comprehensive review of the credit history for each applicant will be undertaken which will include a credit search on all applicants.

Many of the mainstream buy to let lenders will not consider any application where there is evidence of poor credit such as county court judgements, defaults or arrears on any loan. Most lenders use credit-scoring systems when they judge your eligibility for a mortgage by using one of the credit reference agencies such as Equifax and Experian. These agencies don't determine your credit, they just store the information. You can check your own credit rating by contacting either Equifax or Experian.

Your credit record can be impaired by any of the following:

- County Court Judgments (CCJs)

- Mortgage arrears

- Repossessions

- Bankruptcy

- Being in receipt of income benefits

- Unemployment

- Not having a bank account

If you have some adverse credit history, you may still be able to find lenders willing to deal with you; some only deal through brokers. You may have to be prepared to pay a higher rate of interest. Essentially, you will be considered a sub-prime borrower and it is becoming more difficult for such borrowers to obtain a mortgage with the credit crunch conditions in 2008.

If you are self-employed or working on a sub-contract basis, some lenders will require you to have been trading in your present business for a minimum of 3 years. Accounts for the 3 years together with an accountant's reference will be required.

Some lenders make a distinction between novice investors with less than three properties and portfolio landlords with three or more properties who also have more than 12 months lettings experience.

If you are a novice investor, you may feel more comfortable with a lender who will not treat you less favourably than the more seasoned investor.

If you are a portfolio investor, it is worth noting that some lenders may offer you a facility arrangement whereby they agree in principle to let you borrow, say, half a million pounds within the next six months. This has advantages because, although the initial form filling and supporting documentation required are quite cumbersome, the process subsequently is far easier. You can submit the application for the facility arrangement before having any particular properties in mind to buy. Once you have the arrangement in place it will (a) effectively act as an agreement in principle and (b) mean that you only need to submit an abbreviated form for the actual property or properties you wish to buy; this will be both quicker to submit and to process when you want to move quickly to buy a property.

Before I continue to look at the parameters of borrowing and further mortgage features, it should be noted that if you are looking to invest in commercial property (such as offices, shops, factories or other commercial buildings), you will generally need to go to a different set of lenders. It would also be advisable to choose a broker who specialises in the commercial area. The parameters of borrowing will be quite different too.

Top 25 Mortgage Questions to Ask

Below is a list of questions you might want to discuss with your broker when choosing the best lender for your circumstances:

1. **What deals does the lender currently offer?** These can be updated daily. Do remember that the headline rate of interest is not the only worthwhile consideration.

2. **Are there some deals that are only available through mortgage brokers?** The answer may be "yes"; some of the main buy to let lenders prefer to work with brokers as they find in many cases that it is more time efficient.

3. **Do they lend to limited companies?** Obviously one of the first questions you need to ask if you wish to buy as a limited company. You should also ask whether they require personal guarantees (which most of them will).

4. **How does the amount I may borrow relate (if at all) to my personal income?** Many lenders will only consider your rental income when offering a mortgage, while others will take into account your normal income. Lenders may stipulate a minimum income, particularly if you are a new or first-time landlord. They want to know that you can meet all your personal financial commitments. Some lenders may place more emphasis on your earnings than the rent.

5. **What are the lower and upper age limits for borrowers?** For example, some lenders have a lower age limit of 25 years and mortgage terms that are to expire by the borrower's 65th birthday, with a minimum mortgage term of five years.

6. **How many individuals may be named on a mortgage application?** (Normally up to four).

7. **Does the lender exclude from buy to let borrowing, first time buyers or those with no principal primary residence?**

8. **Is there a limit to the number of properties I can buy with the lender?**

9. **Does the lender require me to use a letting agent, or will they allow**

me to manage my own property? It amazed me to find when we began looking into mortgages, that some lenders actually do require you to use a letting agent!

10. **What limits do they set for the type of properties they will lend on:** For example, do they lend on ex-council houses or flats?

11. **Do they allow tenants on benefits such as the new Local Housing Allowance?** Some do not.

Our third investment property - an ex-local authority property
(similar to many we have bought subsequently and let to tenants on benefits)

12. **What criteria must be met in respect of construction (for example, pre-fabricated buildings)?**

13. **Do they lend on high-rise flats?** Many lenders stipulate a maximum of four floors.

14. **What is the lender's minimum property valuation, as well as minimum loan?** £25,000 is the minimum that any mortgage can legally be.

15. **Does the lender impose restrictions on the borrowing if the property needs extensive repairs or renovation before it can be let out?** The lender's valuation officer will decide this. Generally, the lender may keep a retention on part of the loan until any necessary work is completed. This amount will probably be equal to the estimated cost of works. It is important to take this into account if you're thinking of buying a property not immediately suitable for renting out.

16. **What period will the lender apply to the buy to let mortgage regarding the property being in a fit condition to let out?** (For example, eight weeks).

17. **What is the maximum total borrowing possible with the lender?** Some lenders may stipulate a maximum number of properties. The main buy to let lenders tend to stipulate maximum borrowing in money terms, for example £2,000,000. Ask whether this is negotiable.

18. **What redemption penalty applies to the mortgage, particularly during any special rate period?** It is preferable to get a mortgage where the redemption penalty period does not extend beyond the period of any special rate.

19. **Under what circumstances may capital repayments be made?** Usually not during a special rate period?

20. **What is the amount of the lender's arrangement fees for the mortgage?** These can be quite high and it is VERY IMPORTANT to take the cost of any arrangement fee into account.

21. **Are there any other hidden costs involved in arranging the mortgage?** For example, the much maligned MIG - mortgage indemnity premium; luckily not common with buy to let mortgages. You need to be very careful to ascertain that there are no nasty surprises with your mortgage, in terms of hidden costs.

22. **Does the lender have a reasonable application form and reasonable requests for further supporting information?** You do not want to be digging out your school report from when you were five!

23. **How long does the lender generally take to process applications?** As an investor, you should care about your reputation for being able to act quickly; if the lender is slow, this does not help you.

24. **How easy is the lender likely to be to contact?** Some lenders may be remarkably difficult to contact after receiving your initial application.

25. **Are there any further features of the mortgage on offer that are of real value to me, and not merely gimmicky or irrelevant?** Lenders may offer various incentives which are of little intrinsic value and it is important that you do not allow yourself to be side-tracked by them.

Portfolio Building - Releasing Equity for Further Purchases

A very important further consideration is whether the lender allows for drawing further equity from the property without the need for a total re-mortgage. This facility may have different names: for example, it may be called a capital drawdown facility; or a further advance; while other lenders may describe it as an equity release facility.

Being able to release further equity (by whatever name) from property when it increases in value is **key** to enabling you to buy further properties.

This is normally simple and quick process and confirmation of the drawdown can be with you in as little as two weeks, the offer being valid for up to six months. Solicitors and their fees are not required when you release further equity from your property using the same lender, as opposed to a re-mortgaging.

This facility is a **vital feature** to look for in a lender if you wish to build a portfolio of properties.

When you apply for a drawdown, the lender's surveyor will contact you regarding access to the property. It is a good idea for you to meet the surveyor personally for the property valuation assessment. The surveyor may ask what you think the property is now worth. I always make sure I am ready with a decisive answer, pointing out, when possible, similar properties currently for sale or recently sold for the same value. The surveyor is usually grateful for the tip which he can follow up later, as this makes his job easier.

Having done many drawdowns, I have developed trust with our usual surveyors. However, occasionally a different firm of surveyors may be called upon by the lender (at particularly busy times) and they may be from outside the immediate area and so less accurate in their valuations. If the valuation given is lower than you believe it should be, you can dispute this with the lender by sending comparables such as details of properties currently for sale of the same type at the higher value you know to be accurate.

One tip worth noting is to remember to leave some borrowing capacity unused with lender number one, before moving on to lender number two. This means that you will have the borrowing capacity still available for drawing further equity from these earlier properties with lender one, for buying more properties with lender two.

Business Plans

Will you need to submit a business plan with your mortgage application? Generally, the answer should be "no", particularly if you are a new borrower simply looking to buy your first investment property.

However, there may be circumstances where you are required to submit a business plan (depending on the lender), for example if:

- You are a new investor, but wish to gain a large portfolio rapidly

- You have a case to prove, for example if you have previous bad credit

- Your borrowing requirements have reached quite dizzy heights. When I reached the point of asking for more than a million pounds of borrowing from Paragon Mortgages a few years ago, I had to submit a business plan and they sent one of their managers to meet me in person

- If you are applying for a mortgage as a limited company, you may be required to submit a business plan

Submitting a Business Plan

I include in Appendix IV a copy of a Business Plan and Appendix V shows a Cash Flow Forecast that we were requested to supply to the lender, so that you may examine a real example that has actually been used to secure borrowing.

Choose Your Insurance

I include here a discussion of the main insurances that most people will require or consider when buying investment property. The subject of insurance is closely linked with arranging your mortgage, because you will at least be required to have buildings insurance in place as a condition of your mortgage borrowing. Following on from this, mention is made of some further insurance that you may consider relevant or worthwhile, as a landlord.

Insurance is often arranged at the time of arranging the mortgage and this may be done through your IFA. Some lenders offer or require that you use their insurances. You may choose to use an insurance broker, either locally or online, to find competitively priced insurance deals. Ask other landlords who you network with.

If you belong to a landlords' association, you may find they can arrange a discount rate on insurance for members.

Insurance is potentially a big financial burden and rates vary considerably. It is worth asking around to ensure you get the best deal. I recently found a better insurance rate through asking around my contacts.

With any insurance, there is normally an excess, which is the amount of money that you must pay out when you make an insurance claim. The higher the excess, the lower the premiums. Most insurers allow you to choose the excess (within limits) to suit what you feel comfortable with.

Some companies such as www.letsure.co.uk offer buy to let insurance as well as other services to landlords, such as a tenant vetting service.

If you plan to use a letting agent, ask whether their terms and conditions offer any inclusive insurance for landlords: they do sometimes offer an element of rent guarantee or other insurance for landlords.

Buildings Insurance

Buildings insurance covers you in case anything happens to the building itself, for example if it burns to the ground. Premiums for buildings insurance are based on £x amount per £1,000 rebuild cost of the property (as given by the surveyor on the property valuation report) as well as the postcode and claims history. The rebuild cost is not the same as the property value - it is often less, but it can be more.

In the case of leasehold properties or blocks of flats, there is often a block insurance policy which will already be in place. Your solicitor will arrange for your ownership to be noted on the block policy at completion (from which time you will pay for the insurance) and often the lender will also require their interest to be noted. In the case of a house, you will need to arrange the buildings insurance.

Some lenders may require you take out their compulsory insurance policy, which may be more or less competitive.

The insurance arranged must be suitable for a let property. Some insurers won't offer you buildings cover if you are letting to people they deem to be high risk tenants. Such tenants may include students, a group of single people living in a property together, or tenants receiving benefits. Cover for such tenants will probably cost more.

With a portfolio of freehold properties, consider getting a block insurance deal which covers them all under one policy. This is often competitively priced and is also easy to add to when buying new properties. We have a block insurance policy for all our houses.

Contents Insurance

Contents insurance is optional but worth considering, as it can cover not just damage to furniture, fixtures and fittings, but also damage caused by them. If your tenants or their guests are injured by anything from tripping over a carpet to being burnt by a faulty switch, such accidents may result in expensive compensation claims. Contents cover may be either a limited or full policy. A limited policy may be suitable for an unfurnished or part furnished property. A full policy may be preferred for a fully furnished property.

Home contents insurance is something your tenants should get and pay for themselves in respect of cover for losses to their personal property.

Rent Guarantee Insurance

Rent guarantee insurance pays out if your tenant defaults on the rental payments. Policies tend to guarantee rent for a fixed period, usually 6 to 12 months. Premiums may be on a fixed cost policy or more usually calculated as a percentage of the annual rent (around 3%-4%). Such insurance is not compulsory - you must weigh up whether you feel the added peace of mind is worth the extra cost of the insurance.

Life Assurance

Life assurance is not normally compulsory in respect of buy to let properties, unless it is a condition of the mortgage repayment arrangements, as some mortgage terms may require. This should be discussed with your lender, independent financial advisor or your solicitor as required.

Further Insurance Which May be Considered Where Relevant

Legal Expenses

If you get into a disagreement with your tenants and it gets to the stage of legal action, you could find yourself seriously out of pocket. Legal expense cover could help you with collecting unpaid rent, evictions and other potential landlord/tenant disputes.

Public Liability

This covers you against an injury claim by a member of the public, including your tenants.

Personal Accident

May be useful particularly if you intend managing the property yourself, as it will cover you and any joint owner in the property if you are injured whilst there.

Planned Maintenance & Repair or Emergency Assistance

If there is a maintenance problem at the property for which you need to call a specialist to sort out, their services will not be cheap. A good emergency assistance policy will not only pay out on any claims up to a certain figure, but will also organise someone to fix the problem.

Whilst ideally everyone would like to insure against all eventualities, insurance can be expensive and can become simply unaffordable after a point. Buildings insurance is normally the only compulsory insurance and it is for individuals to decide what other insurances to take out.

Once you have found the best lender and mortgage for you and decided on the insurances you want to take out, you should get an agreement in principle from the mortgage lender, ideally from your mortgage broker. It will definitely strengthen your position as a buyer when you can confirm that you have your finances lined up for the purchase.

So now it is time to go ahead and choose your property.

Chapter 6

Choose Your Property

"Do not follow where the path may lead. Go instead where there is no path and leave a trail."
Ralph Waldo Emerson

I am still buying investment property because I know I can run it profitably; because I can buy at below market value, giving a margin of safety; and because I'm confident property is a good long-term investment that also provides income, as long as you know how to keep expenses down.

Choosing your investment property can be exciting, but you must keep a cool business head. Choosing your property well is the very crux of the matter for property investors - buying right is the key to your success. So get ready to buy the right property for you and then you can break open the champagne!

Approach property buying in a serious and professional manner, never forgetting you are an **investor** looking to make a **profit**. Bring yourself back to thinking "it's all about the money" all the time; about yields; about whether you will get an 85% mortgage, preferably with the scope to draw further equity for expanding your portfolio later.

You need to consider your investment goals and ask yourself questions such as:

- **Do I intend to manage or maintain the property myself?** (To be further discussed in the next chapter). This will have a bearing on the location or distance from your home that you will consider buying in.

- **What is my budget?** I allow about £2,500 for purchase costs on an average price property (circa £150,000). This includes 1% stamp duty at £1,500 and solicitors' fees, valuation fees and all necessary searches.

- **What type of property is right for my plans?** This may partly depend on whether you will self-manage; whether you want to undertake refurbishment; whether you are buying to sell or to let; and on how you want the property set up - as a House of Multiple Occupation, for example; or for conversion to flats.

Buying even one property is often the biggest financial decision many people ever make. Buying more than one property is a very big step and it is right to treat it with suitable respect. Hopefully you have not arrived at this point without first going through the several stages of preparation, detailed in the previous chapters, that it is so important to master first. By the time you have finished this chapter, you should be ready to go out and buy your investment property with confidence.

Finding Your Niche

It is important in property investing, as in any business, to recognise that your success will depend on the one hand upon learning as much as you can from the success of those who have gone before you and, on the other hand, using your creativity and powers of lateral thinking to find your own niche. There is merit in becoming an expert in a small niche position. As more and more people join the growing number of property investors, this will become increasingly evident.

I know what works best for us and generally stick to a fairly simple repetition when it comes to choosing our properties. I call this our cookie cutter principle. I fully appreciate that each of us must formulate our own way and that is why I have offered as wide and balanced a view of property investing as possible.

If you think it sounds difficult to go off the beaten track to discover your own niche, do bear in mind that when you find the unique formula that works best for you, all you need do is stick to it. You can make your own uniquely shaped cookie cutter and then use it again and again!

> ## *"Life is either a daring adventure or nothing."*
> ### Helen Keller

Buying locally is our choice and priority as we self-manage our properties and we enjoy the lifestyle and control over our business this allows, but I do appreciate this may not necessarily suit everyone. You will consider your own skills and motivations, as well as other personal factors.

Whether you decide it is for you or not, it must be acknowledged that managing your own properties has a major positive impact for those who do so - on the profitability, the cash flow and the net income. If you can manage your properties yourself and especially if you have reasonable do-it-yourself skills to help you avoid having to rely totally on tradesmen, the ability this gives you to keep expenses down could make all the difference to the profitability of your property business.

Buying locally also gives you the peace of mind of knowing you are readily available for your tenants and your properties. Dave has been able to give up his day job to live off the income from our properties, which would not have been possible if we were paying for the properties to be fully managed and relying on tradesmen for all the maintenance work. This decision needs to be weighed up against your own current circumstances, your abilities, lifestyle choices and so on. You may decide, like many investors I know, that your time is more profitably spent on other things than fixing up properties, particularly if your aptitude or inclinations are not in that area.

Excerpt from Dave's Diary...

Friday 23rd April, 2004:
I collected the rent from 51B.

Sunday 25th April, 2004:
Started working on installing the new water tank at 51B. I drained the system down, disconnected all the pipe work and removed the old water tank, put the new one in place and connected the pipe work. I then had to leave it overnight, for the sealant to dry. So overnight they didn't have any hot water, but they could use the shower and they didn't have any cold water, except at the downstairs loo and the kitchen. I also fixed a kitchen drawer at 51B that was coming apart.

Consider the Location - Where Should You Buy?

NEVER buy in an area that you don't know well or, if you do, use a very trustworthy finder to help you choose a property and who is well aware of your requirements. Buying in an area you don't know well brings additional potential problems. You must do your research very carefully until you can say you do know the area well!

Of primary importance for any area, questions you may need to consider include:

- Is there good tenant demand for rental property in the area?

- Are property prices rising in the area you are considering purchasing in?

- Are there good long-term prospects for the area you are considering purchasing in?

- Are there any regeneration programmes in operation in the area?

Assuming your aim is buy to let, tenant demand in the area and for the type of property you wish to buy is very important. How do you research the demand? You could start by asking several local letting agents. Perhaps place a dummy advertisement in a local paper, or look in local papers and try phoning a few ads from a paper that is a week or two old, to see if the properties are still available. Make a note of 'to let' boards - how long do they stay 'to let'? Be sure to get a realistic assessment of the rent you can expect.

It is a good idea when comparing areas you are considering buying in, to look for the following comparisons:

- Average rental yields

- Average time taken to let a property

- Properties let in six weeks or less

- Property types let

- Tenant profile

- Tenant age group

Think about the characteristics of the area you are considering in terms of rates of employment, average income, public transport and hospitals. Is the area growing or declining? Is the area too reliant on a single employer or industry? Is there a university? Are any major new developments planned, or perhaps government subsidies? Consider the schools and the catchment areas; shopping and local leisure; parking; hospitals and other socio-economic factors.

A good website for looking up more information about the profile of a chosen area is www.upmystreet.com. For my home town, research data on the site regarding our shopping habits reveals a high level of sales of mineral water, low sales of beef burgers and the favourite alcoholic drinks were white wine and port. In the town where we have a lot of investment properties, the favourite drink is lager and there are high-level sales of beef burgers and dog food!

In the area where we primarily buy, there is a lively airport which attracts a lot of contract workers, many from other countries. Contract workers and people new to the country are more inclined to rent properties and this means there is a good demand for rental property. What are the particular features of the area/s you are considering?

What Tenants Want

It pays to be aware when choosing property of what tenants want. Here are the findings of a survey on what tenants look for when choosing a property to rent:

- Most tenants were concerned with location: 72.5% of tenants said that location was one of the most important features to them when choosing a property to rent.

- The next most important features quoted were size of rooms (37%)

- Parking (37%)

- Quality fixtures and fittings (37%)

- Whether the property was furnished or unfurnished (35%)

- More tenants were concerned about whether the property was modern (30%)

- Or had character (23%)

- Than whether or not it had a garden or outdoor space (21%)

- More people wanted a good quality kitchen (31%)

- Than a good quality bathroom (22%)

- 25% required a shower

- And 31% were looking for a property with cheap rent

- Only 7% said they wanted a property where they could keep a pet

- And the least demanded feature was a garage (5%).

- Most tenants viewed three or fewer properties before choosing one (48%) and, of these, 30% chose the first property they saw.

- A significant minority (18%) looked at more than 10 properties before choosing the one they now rent.

- Although only 16% of the tenants questioned said it was important to them that the property was decorated to their taste, when asked what they would change about their rented property, most mentioned they would change some aspect of the décor - for example, the colour of the wallpaper, carpets or furniture.

Target Tenant Profile as Part of Property Choice

Don't just choose a property that you would like to live in. You may prefer to live in a quiet street near to a good school, happy to drive into town to shop. But many tenants may be younger* and prefer somewhere lively, close to amenities such as shops, restaurants and pubs. They may require close proximity to public transport links.

* Did you know that the average age of the property investor is 46, while the average age of tenants is 26?

On the other hand, don't make narrow assumptions about your tenants and who they might be. It is important to research the actual tenant base for the area and property type you wish to invest in, before you buy your property. Talk to local letting agents. You should be clear about your target tenants and their needs and requirements.

The main categories of tenants you can expect and the type of property likely to suit the target group are outlined below. Of course, when you get your property you may happen to attract any individual tenant not necessarily in the target or 'stereotypical' group, which is fine. These definitions are designed to guide rather than define.

Students: They will require property as close to campus as possible and close to local amenities including shops, public transport and a pub. Students will appreciate a lower rent more than a state of the art kitchen or bathroom. A big (perhaps old) property with lots of rooms is ideal for students sharing. The lounge may be considered for a bedroom (preferably where a sizeable kitchen/diner exists). You will need to check whether your mortgage lender allows for students. Also consider what regulations apply if you are setting up a house of multiple occupation (this will be discussed further later in this chapter).

Remember that renting to students is a niche market and requires careful planning and consideration. Among the factors to be considered are that students' lives move on quickly and they are generally not around during a long summer period; also they do not have much money and are not in stable family units.

If you have children heading off to university, it is worth noting that some people choose to buy a property in the town where their child goes to university. Your child could benefit from reduced rent, while keeping an eye on other students sharing the property.

Professionals: Typically young working people in their 20's; this is the most common type of tenant in the UK. I asked a letting agent: "How do you define 'professional' tenants?" and he said: "Anyone who's got a job, really!" You may want to be a bit more specific about the people you aim to attract to rent your property. I don't think it is unreasonable, for example, to ask prospective tenants how much they earn, to gauge how affordable the property is for them.

If you are likely to get sharers, try to choose properties with evenly sized bedrooms, particularly for two bedroom flats or houses. Sometimes these have been designed with a young family in mind, the second bedroom being noticeably smaller than the master one.

Many working people, or professionals, will require a newly decorated place with neutral tones and at least kitchen appliances provided.

The Corporate Tenant: It is particularly important to establish that there is a good current and stable demand in the area for company lets. This type of market tends to thrive mainly in big cities. Note that big companies will almost certainly only deal with letting agents and the required standards throughout the property will be very high. Yields can be relatively low. Landlords can be vulnerable to company cutbacks and relocations.

City centre properties tend to be expensive, but it can be a good idea to buy property just outside major cities that have reliable transport links into the city. If you are really interested in the corporate market, check the demand for properties 'on the outskirts'. Around London and many other big cities, it is not only cheaper to buy property that is outside the central areas, but also widens your pool of potential tenants. Towns that are easily commutable to London also have their own infrastructure and tenants may work locally or commute to London.

Families: When we began buying three bedroom houses, we envisaged nice families moving in but were surprised at the low percentage of these we found as tenants. As a group, families are more likely to either buy their own homes or be eligible for council or housing association properties. Now we find tenants via the council and do get families. Some families rent temporarily in the course of moving to a new town (often with the financial support of an employer). Some also choose to rent privately and then claim benefits, if they have been unhappy with properties offered by the council directly, or there is a shortage of council housing. You would need to check with your lender and insurance company whether benefit claimants are permitted.

If you do hope to target families, choose good-sized accommodation with a good kitchen and plenty of storage, in quiet streets near to schools and nurseries, with enclosed gardens.

The picture above shows one of our properties where a family live as tenants. Isn't it ironic that this property, along with countless others, was once owned by the council, housing council tenants who paid a very low rent while the council had the benefit of ownership? Many of these properties, after being sold, ended up in the hands of private landlords just in time for the boom years (so we ended up with the capital gain) and we now house tenants claiming benefits from the council for a rent far in excess of what the council themselves were once charging. But ours is not to question why!

We now work with the local council which has the role of finding housing for families currently living in temporary accommodation due to a shortage of council housing in the area, and most of our tenants are found this way.

Trend Spotting

Some investors make trend spotting the focus of their investment decisions, at least initially. This worked well for Judith Wilson and her husband, a couple of maths teachers who went on to buy over £100 million worth of property and have a place in the Times Rich List. They bought around 700 properties to let in Kent in the area when plans were in progress for the area's rejuvenation based largely on the Channel Tunnel terminal being built.

I enjoyed watching a TV documentary about the Wilsons a few years ago and I also cut out their story from the newspaper and stuck it on the wall by my telephone. Another reason I liked their story is that her husband admitted it was Judith who masterminded their investment strategy, so one up for the ladies!

My favourite bit about their story was how they told of spending £6.9 million on property in one afternoon when an interest rate cut was announced. They had worked out mathematically in anticipation of the rate cut that they would be able to do this. I think the lesson we all need to learn is this:

- Remember when choosing property that you are investing money

- It's all about the money

- It is good to boil it all down to the figures

- To remain suitably detached and focused on what you are aiming at: making lots of money

Buying Ex-Council Property

A high percentage of the properties we own are ex-local authority (ex-LA) properties. Our neighbouring town, where many of our properties are, was created as a 'new town' in the late 60's/early 70's, with mainly social housing being built by the government commission responsible for this social engineering. In the 80's, Margaret Thatcher brought in the 'right to buy' for council tenants and now some 80%-90% per cent of the houses in this town are privately owned, the figure being somewhat less for flats: 50% overall with wider variations depending on the particular location.

These ex-LA properties, which can be found in all towns and regions, offer good value to buy and a good rental yield for buying to let in particular.

The properties are often solidly built, with generous proportions and sensible family layouts. As with any purchase, you should do your own due diligence with regard to the area the property is in. Be prepared to put personal views aside though; the key thing is whether the property will let easily for a good rental yield.

Considering Different Types of Property

When buying a house, I find that three bedroom terrace houses offer better value for money to buy and also give a better yield on the rent than two bedroom houses, in my area. They also offer good value for tenants, especially when they are ex-council properties.

Traditional wisdom in property investing has been that smaller properties offer better yields than larger properties. However, this does not always hold true with the one bedroom flat, depending on the area and market conditions at the time. In my area, one-bedroom flats generally do not offer such good value.

One of the big decisions or choices to be made is whether to buy a freehold property (generally a house) or leasehold property (generally a flat). I currently have 42 houses and 19 flats. I used to buy flats and houses in equal measure, but now favour houses as I generally find they are more profitable because of the absence of service charges. (It should be noted that in Scotland flats are generally freehold, so the situation is different).

If you are not available to manage your own properties, you may feel that flats have an advantage, however, in requiring less maintenance by the owner - at least in terms of the exterior of the building and grounds. Although, to be fair, we do not find those parts of our freehold properties take up much time.

Houses in Multiple Occupation (HMOs)

If you want to let a property to a group of unrelated people, the property will probably be considered a House in Multiple Occupation (an HMO).

The legal definition of a house in multiple occupation is, briefly, 'a house which is occupied by persons who do not form a single household' The term also includes any purpose-built or converted flat whose occupants do not form a single household. The definition is not precise; a large number of premises could potentially be considered HMOs.

There are various categories of HMO including: bedsits; student accommodation; hostels and guest houses; old people's homes and the like.

HMO Licensing legislation was implemented nationally in 2006, under regulations laid down in the Housing Act 2004. Under these regulations, all HMOs are subject to management regulations and codes of practice and to breach these is a criminal offence. But not all HMOs need to be licensed. There are three types of licensing: mandatory, selective and additional. Licensing fees vary between authorities and a license can last for up to five years.

The government has implemented mandatory licensing to HMOs with three or more storeys and five or more persons, living in more than one 'household' (i.e. family unit).

Local authorities have additional powers to license properties excluded from mandatory licensing:

- Selective licensing may be applied to properties in low demand areas; or where anti-social behaviour problems are common.

- They may also impose additional licensing on individual HMOs (or properties belonging to a particular landlord), which are causing problems.

In Scotland, HMO licensing was introduced earlier than in England and regulations have been strictly implemented. Many former HMO investors quit the market when these new regulations and associated costs came in, although others see this as an opportunity, due to reduced competition.

From a landlord's point of view, HMOs can be attractive as more profit can be gained from the property than by letting out the same as a single household. If you are interested in letting property as an HMO, bear in mind the layout, or potential layout, of the property for this purpose.

We own several three bedroom terraced houses with similar layouts. The internal layout of these houses varies in two or three ways only, though the overall size and price of them is basically the same. Some of the properties have an open-plan lounge with a smaller kitchen and others have a self-contained lounge with a larger kitchen/diner. The latter style is much better suited for an HMO, because the lounge can be used as a fourth bedroom, while the tenants have a comfortable sized kitchen/diner in which to cook, eat and congregate.

Making changes to a property in order to create an HMO is further addressed below under the section Consider Whether to Refurbish.

HMOs can be attractive from the tenants' point of view, too. For single people, this sort of accommodation can be a relatively cheap and attractive option. The downside, from the landlord's point of view, can be that people in this situation are often more mobile, with lives in a fluid and transitory state. This fluidity can mean a high turnover of tenants, which in itself is hard work. Problems can also arise if the sharers do not get along together and seek to entangle you in their disputes (which you may find unavoidable); though I do find this can happen at properties where any group, even a family, have taken up residence!

Accreditation for Landlords and their Premises

Linked to the new licensing regulations, accreditation schemes are available to landlords. Accreditation involves adherence to a set of standards (or code) relating to the management or physical condition of privately rented accommodation. Landlords who join a scheme and abide by the standards are 'accredited'. Accreditation schemes are voluntary.

I became an accredited landlord myself after attending an accreditation course which was very informative, and especially useful in getting to grips with the myriad new government regulations that landlords need to abide by since the new Housing Act came into force.

There is no compulsion for landlords to join an accreditation scheme but there may be advantages, such as the availability of reduced licensing fees for HMOs, grants available only to accredited landlords, and access to some tenant groups. Some local authorities are working with local universities, for example, to ensure their students only rent property from accredited landlords.

If you are interested in becoming an accredited landlord, ask at your local council. Schemes are often run by the Housing or Environmental Health Department. Or visit www.anuk.org.uk for further information.

Buying Leasehold Property

If you are thinking of buying a flat in England or other leasehold property, consider the following facts:

Ten Facts about Leasehold

1. In 2008 Leasehold is still the only way to 'own' a flat, (sometimes a house) in England and Wales.

2. Leaseholders do NOT actually own the property; they just have permission - subject to conditions - to live there for the time left on the lease.

3. Leaseholders buy a time period, not a property.

4. The actual property owner is a freeholder, who is also in charge of any major decisions.

5. Lessees pay the freeholder for the upkeep of the building.

6. The less time left on the lease, the less it's worth, because it has to be returned to the freeholder, who sells it again.

7. When their lease ends, their home is still physically there but lessees have to leave, or may rent back from the freeholder but without any long-term security.

8. As time passes, maintenance of the building and services often costs more. The leaseholder pays for this, but on the freeholder's orders.

9. As time passes the lease gets shorter, and a leasehold property loses value in two ways: it costs more to maintain, and the freeholder can charge more to lengthen the lease.

10. There are more than two million leaseholds in England. The numbers are increasing daily, in many areas at a faster rate than freehold properties.

For leasehold properties, you should also consider the following points:

- You will not only pay for maintenance work, but also have very little control over what work is done (other than in a very small block).

- The consent of a lender may be required to rent out your property and failure to obtain such consent may make your mortgage or insurance invalid. Make sure you find out if buy to let tenants are allowed before even offering on the property.

- Flats situated in England will usually have a freeholder who will also need to give consent. Again, check this out before offering on the flat.

- Check what the level of service charge is (although it will vary each year), when it is payable and what the service charge covers. The quoted service charge may be more or less inclusive of the following: building insurance; reception or security staff (if relevant); upkeep of grounds and lifts if any; interior and exterior maintenance; cleaning and heating of communal areas.

- You and your solicitor will get a copy of the lease at some stage during the purchase process (try to get this sooner rather than later, if you have any concerns). Your solicitor will help to advise you of any details that may be of concern.

- Check whether there is a tenants' association or management company and what kind of responsibilities you would be expected to take on. At one of our blocks, we get fined if we do not attend the AGM.

- Some leasehold properties will have a short lease. Mortgage lenders normally require the lease to have at least 40 years left by the end of the mortgage term (as it stands at the time of purchase). A relatively short lease should be reflected in a lower purchase price than a similar property with a longer lease. Leaseholders do have the right in law to an extension of the lease term, although the costs and terms of this vary widely. Other complications arise, such as the management committee for the block trying to get agreement from all leaseholders to secure a good deal for the lease extension, which may not always be forthcoming.

- If you are considering the purchase of a flat that has a short lease term remaining (anything less than 70 years) check firstly whether this is acceptable to your lender. It is also important to research the cost of having the lease extended. The cost may be anywhere from £2,000 to over £20,000, depending on the freeholder, as well as the lease length remaining and other factors. You may be able to ascertain from local estate agents experienced in selling other flats in the block whether the cost of extending the lease matches with the selling price of others where the lease has been extended.

- Where owners make arrangements individually to extend the lease, the cost is often higher than if this is done as a group. It can be worthwhile asking whether other leaseholders in the block are interested in getting together to try and get a discount on the cost of extending.

- It can be worthwhile buying a flat with a short lease if the value will increase by more than the cost of having it lengthened. For example, we own a flat where plans are underway to get the lease extended at a cost per flat of £7,000. Identical flats where the lease has already been lengthened sell for £14,000 more.

Splitting Freehold Properties into Leasehold Units

In some areas, it is not uncommon to find large old properties that have been converted into separate flats and which may have been let out as separate flats for several years but there is still just one freehold title. It is possible to buy such properties and arrange to split the freehold into separate leasehold units. This need not necessarily involve any extra work being done to the property, but can effectively increase the value by up to 50%. The leasehold properties can then be re-mortgaged, thus releasing cash from the arrangement.

Consider Whether to Refurbish

You may wish to specifically target properties in need of refurbishment so that you can add value, or you may simply be prepared to accept that properties which come cheap may be in need of a little TLC. Ask yourself in advance what you are prepared to take on board, bearing in mind whether you need to let the place out.

What you need to know is that the increase in the property's value will be more than the cost of the work.

Increase in value minus cost of work = added value

You should aim to add only the value required to let the property out or to sell at a worthwhile profit, if that is your intention. Do not waste your time or money on unnecessary work purely because it is 'pretty', or fun to do!

While the work you consider worth undertaking is a matter for personal choice, you should bear in mind that you are losing potential rent during the time taken to do any work. When letting is the aim, I suggest you only do work that adds to the rent achievable.

Say, for example, you want to add an en-suite shower, pause to consider:

- Will this really mean you can charge more rent for the property?

- Will it mean the property is valued higher than the cost of the work, when you want to release further equity later?

- How long will it take to do the work and be able to let the place out?

- If the main benefit will be to make the property more attractive when selling, would it be better to leave the work until the time of sale, so it will be freshly done?

Do bear in mind that, at the time of purchase, you only have to provide a 15% deposit, whereas for any subsequent work you will have to provide 100% of the funds required.

My policy is to go for properties in need of some simple tender loving care, which I can provide myself! By this, I mean properties that are below average price for their type simply because they are scruffy and in need of new carpets or in bad decorative order, maybe from smelly pets or dressed in 1970s fashions. They may not have double glazing or radiator central heating (but many do still have the old warm air systems which are adequate). These things make the property cheaper to buy, but do not necessarily impact on the rent achievable or the tenants' comfort. They can be upgraded later as or when desired.

One scenario worth considering is making alterations to a property that will make it suitable for use as a HMO, as this can greatly increase the income or cash flow from the property. Works that are required will obviously depend on any changes to layout and room use you may wish to make, but will also depend on such factors as whether the property will be licensable and also on the specific regulations of the local council. Most local councils' websites will be a good starting point for further information on this; changes may include the need for planning permission, building regulations consent and other requirements.

Property Development

The term 'property development' is used when modifications to a property are to be made. While it may be applied loosely to some of the tasks involved in refurbishment, such as fitting a new bathroom suite or kitchen, property development normally implies that more major or structural changes are to be carried out; or indeed that a property will be built from scratch, either on a vacant piece of land or after demolishing another building to create the space.

Developing property requires serious and careful planning and is bound to involve putting together a winning team that should include an architect and builders, project manager (which could be you, if you understand all that's involved in the job) as well as financial advisors who can help to structure the finance for the project. Much liaison will be required with the local council, in applying for planning permission and in compliance with building regulations and so on.

When people buy a site with a view to development, they often structure the deal to involve an option to buy that is subject to planning permission being granted. In terms of expected profit, developers often work on allowing roughly one third buy-in cost, to one third development costs, to one third for profit.

Without the strictest of discipline and good estimation over costs and time the project should take, money could easily be lost by going over budget.

One tip for anyone who owns property is to consider for each of your properties whether there may be scope for profitable development. A large or corner plot could be a hidden gem, maybe one that you already own!

Commercial Property

Any type of property, including commercial has, in general historically, been a good investment. Commercial property has traditionally been the reserve of the ultra-wealthy, or of big corporations, and is associated in many people's minds with being out of their financial reach.

It should not be dismissed or overlooked though and can provide a welcome addition to a mixed portfolio. Commercial properties can of course include places worth hundreds of millions of pounds in one building, but could also be more humble premises costing no more than the residential properties we might be buying.

Buy Below Market Value

This was discussed in detail in the earlier chapter Sourcing and Analysing Below Market Value Property Deals. The present heights of the property market in the

UK, as well as the increasing number of repossessions, provide increasingly ideal conditions for finding below market value bargains. When you buy property, make it your number one rule to get the property at below the current average price being paid for directly comparable properties. This will be a positive first step for many reasons which have already been looked at in detail. In brief:

- It will enable you to expand your portfolio quicker, as the property can be valued up by a greater amount at an earlier date than if you had paid more for it.

- Paying less will give you a margin for error should prices fall back, or if you need to accept a lower rent than you hoped for.

There are always keenly priced properties to be found and with due diligence this can be achieved.

I have always chosen properties that are priced low. Especially when prices have been through a sustained period of fairly rapid growth, it's important not to be left holding an over-priced property.

Even now, I may buy property through an estate agent at £150,000 knowing that the average price for the area (same type) is £170,000. Although this is not a huge discount, I believe it is necessary to keep the idea of buying below market value in perspective, taking account of local market conditions as well as your own circumstances.

When I first learnt about marketing for below market value properties, I turned my back on estate agents' listings completely. However, I did not find as many deals as I had hoped and realised, with hindsight, that, because I had released a quarter of a million pounds from my portfolio I could have gone out and bought a dozen properties at open market value at the beginning of 2006 that would have gone up (with the rising market in my area) by 20% over the course of the year.

In a rising market, today's BMV property is yesterday's OMV property, so if you have the funds to buy it may be worth asking yourself "why wait?"

The biggest lesson I've learnt from this myself is to always be an **independent** thinker. Question everything - even the holy grail of buying BMV, if that is right for you!

Finding Motivated Sellers

Generally speaking though, it is a good idea to look for motivated sellers, wherever they may be. Do remember that you will be providing the solution to their problem when you take the property off their hands quickly and without fuss. This should always be a win/win situation for all parties involved. I find the reasons why a particular property may be cheap include:

- The seller had a buyer and the sale was quite advanced, but the buyer dropped out, threatening the whole chain. They need another buyer who is reliable and can move quickly. In a rising market, they may be aware that local prices have risen since they accepted the figure they did three months ago, but this is of little interest to them; they are prepared to accept an offer of the same amount (now a bargain to the buyer) to preserve the purchase of the property they have their heart set on. If you view a property where everything is packed into boxes, it may be worth asking if the sale fell through!

- Repossessed properties can be well priced for a fast sale, but not necessarily. Sometimes, agents will try to avoid mentioning that a property is repossessed, because they believe this is likely to attract lower offers. When viewing a repossessed property though, there are often tell-tale signs, such as notices and stickers on lavatories saying "do not use"!

- A seller may be under threat of repossession and desperate for a quick sale to avoid financial crisis. Or the seller may have another financial crisis.

- Divorce can be a stressful time for sellers and sometimes the acrimonious feelings leave the property sale price a very low priority for two people keen to get as far away as possible from each other!

- Sometimes a death in the family produces a property that can be purchased for an amount significantly below market value. I know of a house that had been on the market for almost a year because the family could not bring themselves to clear the property. The eventual purchaser arranged to clear the house and worked with one of the family members to place some treasured items with friends of the family. The house was purchased well below market value. A win/win solution.

- Emigrating - sometimes the seller is running out of time and wants to clear everything up before he/she leaves.

- We also quite often find properties at below market value which are for sale by a previous landlord! Don't let this put you off. If you have done your due diligence, you should be confident about your decision to buy property. There will always be landlords who are selling as well.

Often, previously let properties are a bargain because they have not been well lived in. We are very familiar with that certain je ne sais quoi which lets us know tenants are or were there. It may be that certain unloved look: the unkempt garden; the black marks on the walls and light switches; the worn carpets; the mess or even the smell! If tenants are still living at the property for sale, you may want to consider keeping them on. However, don't be surprised if any letting agent involved is keen to move them to a different property managed by themselves.

More Tips and Tricks

If you want to be clever about looking high and low for your property, here are some tips:

- Note properties that are for sale with multiple agents (this can be a sign of the sellers' desperation).

- Some estate agents are frankly not very on the ball, or au fait with the particular type of property.

- Sometimes sellers put their property on for sale with an agent outside the usual catchment area and the agent may be less expert in the property prices for the area.

- If you spot a property that has been for sale for an abnormal length of time, the vendors may be open to low offers. But again, beware - the property may have been over-priced in the first place, or may be part of some domestic hassle. A property local to us was for sale for over a year, which is normally unheard of. I asked a friend about it, and she said the divorced wife who was still living in the property had been ordered by the court to sell, but didn't want to, so just acted awkwardly to put buyers off. It may hardly be worth wasting your time with such a situation.

- Sometimes vendors try to sell their own property by putting a little home-made sign outside. You must always wonder why they don't go to an agent like most people - there just might be a bargain to be had.

- Look out for empty properties and try to find out the circumstances. In rare cases where property has been abandoned, it can be possible to lay claim to ownership if no owner comes forward to claim it (but only after 15 years of possession!)

- You may be feeling energetic and go round leafleting properties, informing the owners that you are a purchaser who can proceed quickly and discreetly, as discussed at length previously.

- You can also put 'property wanted' adverts in local papers or shops, preferably stating you are a 'cash buyer'.

- Try auctions; there are still bargains available but, treat auctions with caution. Many people - particularly investors - have latched on to auctions these days and prices can be pushed up beyond the level they would fetch on the high street. Properties that are for sale at auctions are often not straightforward properties, and may be more difficult to get buy to let finance on anyway.

- And last, but not least, don't forget to mention to everyone you know that you buy property. You never know who might come to you for a quick solution.

- Do not overlook the obvious route of going through estate agents. Let's face it, this is still how most properties are sold. To avoid estate agents could mean overlooking the obvious. There are always some properties that will be favourably priced with agents; property pricing is not an exact science and sellers all have their own situations to cope with.

Preparing for Property Viewing

Before you look at your first property, remember that your offer is more likely to be accepted if you can present yourself as someone who can proceed quickly with the sale. Be sure that you have lined up your finances, and that you have the details of your IFA (or mortgage broker) and solicitor ready to hand over. Show you are keen by arranging to view promptly if possible. When I see a property that I am keen on, I generally try to arrange to view on the same day I phone about it. Often this will be daytime during the week, which is easier for estate agents and fewer other viewers are likely to be able to get along.

If you are an experienced buyer, then say so. If you do put forward an offer for a property, show confidence in your decision - act quickly and decisively. Your perceived professionalism and ability to move ahead effortlessly will encourage sellers to accept your offer in preference to another similar one (even if yours is not the highest).

When I first began investing in property, I registered with all the local estate agents for details of the type of property I was interested in and I also began to train myself to study the local property pages carefully each week. I asked questions and visited some of the blocks of flats where I thought I might buy. I got to know the differences in prices between the various blocks in the town and also their varied reputations. (I now prefer to buy freehold property, as discussed earlier).

It is a good idea to talk to as many estate agents as possible in the area where you wish to buy and arrange to get details sent to you of the type of properties you are interested in. However, don't rely too much on them continuing to send you details. When properties are flying through their doors in a hot market, they simply may not have the time to do this. When you deal with estate agents, remember that they act for the seller and get paid commission by the seller. Don't allow agents to talk you into viewing properties that are not your choice, if you are not happy to do so. You do not want to waste time - time is money.

Keep an eye on the local papers and look at properties on the internet. Many estate agents will have their own individual websites, but many also use bigger sites that can be very informative and full of tips and research information. Properties often get updated daily on the internet, so you can quickly get details of any new ones and you can arrange to get email alerts of properties that fit your requirements. Some of the big property sales sites include:

www.rightmove.co.uk

www.assertahome.com

www.fish-4homes.co.uk

Don't forget to look at more local sites as well and at the rental side of these sites. It is important that you learn to estimate the rent achievable for each type of property you may buy.

One thing I tend to steer away from is glossy property marketing, as I do not feel it goes hand in hand with acquiring a good investment. It is usually associated with newbuild properties, including new properties abroad for which a premium may be paid. Near where I live, there is a shop selling attractive Spanish properties - surely this appeals more to the spender than to the investor? Remember to think independently and question everything - even me saying this!

People may be attracted to new build properties partly because of seemingly favourable finance arrangements that can be offered, such as gifted deposits, first year's rent guaranteed and other schemes. Such properties are often advertised as being available 'at 15% (or even 20%) discount'. Such claims should be treated with caution. If too many investors buy into a new block of flats, they can become difficult to let out and difficult to sell, meaning you will lose money and have to sell for less than the 'supposed' value (which is unproven until the original buyers come to sell). Lenders are now increasingly reluctant to lend on newbuild properties for buy to let, so it seems they agree with me!

As well as location and all considerations of the neighbourhood, the actual state of the properties being viewed is of primary importance. After narrowing down the location and type of property you want to view, you will want to view several in order to choose the best. It is a good idea to write notes during and/or straight after each viewing, so that later you can clearly remember which property had which features. Do not be afraid of taking photographs or even a video of the properties (with the owners' permission).

See Appendix II for a Property Viewing Checklist.

Headaches You May Get When Buying

When buying property, you need to be prepared for the headaches that may be involved in the process. Very often, problems arise which can be worked through and your patience may be required to smooth ruffled feathers. Just remember, if you can keep your head while those around you are losing theirs, you are a born winner!

So what can go wrong?

- Problems can arise with property chains (of buyers and sellers) and this can be helped by those involved remaining level-headed. Your solicitor or other solicitors in the chain may be working too slowly for the liking of some members of the chain. As a buy to let investor, you have two main advantages and as such should be a welcome addition to the chain:

  - Effectively you will normally break or end the chain (as you will not be selling, but only buying).

  - You can normally be flexible about completion dates, as you are not personally moving home.

  - The surveyor may undervalue the property, meaning that you may not get the full amount of mortgage you had hoped for. In this case, you have four possible courses of action open to you:

    1. You could go back to the seller via the agent and let them know that you now wish to revise your offer downwards, as the property has been professionally deemed to be worth less than the originally agreed price. The seller may be happy to comply.

However, they may not be happy to change the price and you may still be keen to continue with the purchase, in which case:

2. If you are confident that the valuer is mistaken, you normally have the right to dispute this through the mortgage lender's proper channels, by submitting details of comparables - comparable properties, at the higher value.

3. If neither of the above produces the desired results, you may decide you can afford to pay the extra amount (which may be a couple of thousand pounds) with the deposit to move ahead with the purchase.

4. Of course, if none of the above is satisfactory, you can always withdraw from the purchase.

- If the vendor wishes to withdraw from selling, try to remain patient and to find out all the reasons for this; it is possible that a new agreement can be reached, if you are very keen to proceed.

- It is possible that you will be gazumped. (This is where a new offer is accepted after yours has already been accepted, usually because it was higher). I have been on the receiving end of this myself, but see little point in getting steamed up about it. I would never engage in putting forward a higher offer again in these circumstances, as I will have lost trust in the seller. Gazumping is legal in England, so we do have to accept it can happen.

- Problems may arise with your mortgage application. Again, this may require sending further information and a little patience can go a long way. Learn to like the music that you get to listen to when you are kept on hold on the telephone and the endless reams of paperwork, and you will be fine!

The Buying Process

With regards to how a property purchase proceeds, there is a buying process for England and Wales and a different process for Scotland, details of which are given in appendices as indicated below:

Appendix VI: The Buying Process for England and Wales

Appendix VII: How the Buying Process Differs in Scotland

It is worth familiarising yourself with the step-by-step process of conveyancing and purchase, as you will then be able to help keep things moving apace by anticipating what needs to be done and ensuring it is done promptly.

Once you have successfully bought, you need to make decisions about managing your property.

Chapter 7

Property Management

"The heights by great men reached and kept were not attained by sudden flight, but they, while their companions slept, were toiling upward in the night."
Henry Wadsworth Longfellow

When we bought our first investment property, we thought mainly about the capital appreciation and the modest income this would yield. We expected to use a letting agent to find and manage tenants for us. We felt that Dave would be capable of dealing with what little property maintenance we expected, in his spare time.

Dave had a full-time job. I had two young children and was pregnant with our third. The rental property was something we saw as being very much in the background of our lives. In fact, by replacing the income from the lodgers we no longer had room for at home, we saw it as an effective reduction in our workload rather than an increase.

We had no inkling at that time that property management would become central to our investment plans, our success and our lives.

Getting an investment property is a bit like a new addition to the family: very welcome and a cause for celebration; lovely when clean, dry and quiet; but are we ever really prepared for the hard work, tears and tantrums that arise along the way?

Whilst many property investors do not manage their own properties, it is worth giving serious consideration to doing so and keeping more of the profits for yourself. In this chapter and the next, as well as examining what property management involves in general terms, I would like to give you an insight into our own experiences, to help you decide whether the choice to do your own property management is right for you.

Firstly then, what is property management? Property management covers at least two main areas:

- Works and maintenance

- Managing your tenants

Ideally before purchasing your property, you should decide whether you might be prepared to personally undertake the property management, or would definitely prefer to employ others to do it for you. As a landlord you may choose to handle both areas yourself or employ others to act for you in one or both of these areas. However, it will only really be practical to manage your own property if it is reasonably local. If you feel you may like to self-manage, then distance from where you live is an important consideration when choosing the property.

In property, as in any business, there are different levels of thinking and doing that must be addressed simultaneously. While Dave mainly chooses to work IN the business, I myself go to work ON the business. It is the working ON the business that drives the business forward, whilst the work that must be done IN the business is essential to its welfare on a daily basis. Both are equally important to the continued success of the business.

The debate can get quite heated about whether it is a good idea to self-manage your properties. I completely understand and respect that to do so is not the right decision for everyone. In our case Dave does much of the maintenance work as well as managing the tenants, which works well for us. It is also a lifestyle choice he made because he enjoys the work and has an aptitude for it.

The following chart shows the decisions to be considered and the choices to be made about whether to manage your own property:

Decision Chart – Do you want to manage your own property?

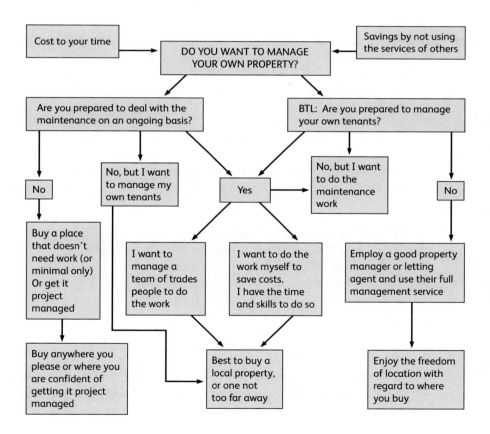

As well as the property location, the time and skills you have available will have a bearing on your decision. As your time is money, it is very important to weigh up the options before making any decisions. Doing as much as possible yourself will enable you to keep more of the profit instead of spending it on the services of others. However, this might not necessarily be the best course of action for you. Other factors may override the possible cost savings that can be achieved by personally doing much of the work. The main factors to be considered are:

1. The best capital appreciation or yield may be gained by buying property not local to where you live. The prospect of great capital gains is beyond your control and there is always a risk that the expected gains will not materialise. You should therefore ensure that you can run the property with a positive cash flow in the meantime.

2. You may be able to earn more money in other ways than the saving you will make by not employing others. For example, if you have the option of employing a decorator for £40 a day, ask yourself whether you should do the work yourself, or whether you can earn more than that doing something else - sourcing new properties perhaps.

3. Your aptitude or interest in gaining experience as a handyman are more important at this stage than your current level of skills. Dave has developed his skills with the maintenance work along the way but I have not! The aptitude and interest are both vital.

Dave's Tip...

 Sometimes a maintenance issue arises that I have not encountered before and don't feel confident to tackle. For example, the first time we had a water tank that became leaky and had to be changed, I employed a plumber to install a new tank but chose one who was willing to allow me to help, which reduced his bill and also enabled me to learn the skill. The next time a tank needed changing I used my new skill to do the job myself, saving us money

---

It is difficult to weigh up the financial impact of paid help as the care and attention, the honesty and efficiency with which work is carried out are all factors to be considered in practice. Our experience has been that nobody else is going to act as quickly, with as much care or as little expense as Dave himself does.

Even if you do much of the work yourself, there are bound to be times when you will need to employ the services of others to help you. Unless you already have reliable contacts, you are likely to have a period of trial and error with regard to finding reliable tradesmen with acceptable fees. At least being in control of which tradesmen you use is usually a good idea, as you can keep the costs down.

It makes sense to try out doing your own property management in the early days, while you still have only one or two properties, perhaps by doing the maintenance side only at first and dealing with tenants when you get more confident (as we did). With only one or two properties, the work should easily fit into your spare time, and this will give you the opportunity to decide if you think you are cut out for developing your business along self-managing lines.

Any work you do yourself will save money and increase your profits. You must be willing to take the time to learn the business in a serious manner and to take good care of your properties. Be sure that you stay committed to the business as time goes by, if you want it to continue to thrive.

As a property investor, you will find the business involves many kinds of work, some mental and some physical. One of the good things about this business is that it lends itself to flexibility over which chores to do yourself or to pay someone else to do according to your inclinations, but remember that whichever jobs you do yourself can save you money and those savings will impact on your profits. Think about which of the following areas you might be willing to do yourself:

- Book-keeping

- Managing tenants and collecting rents

- Setting up new properties ready to rent out

- Cleaning properties between tenancies

- General maintenance work

- Painting inside and out

- Garden clearance

There are always people willing to do these things for you, but they will charge you, often quite dearly. Some professionals charge up to £100 an hour for their labour. Can you afford not to save that expense wherever possible?

We do use some tradesmen regularly, mainly: CORGI gas engineer, qualified electrician and a double glazing man.

However, we prefer not to use tradesmen whenever possible. We once paid a couple of painters £700 to paint an entire house as there was much other work to be done. We thought the cost was justified if it meant the place being ready to rent quicker than we could achieve by working alone. However, the painters took twice as long as promised, by which time we had finished work on other things and could have done it ourselves!

An important necessity in any business is to maintain a positive cash flow and maximise the profits. Doing your own management will help you to achieve this over and over again, and is therefore the best investment you can make in the business. When you do your own repairs you know that they will be done promptly, as cost effectively as possible and to a good standard; the peace of mind this brings is as worthwhile as the cost saving.

If you are unable to do the work yourself, you must consider whether it is worth buying a property that needs work doing, or if you would be better off buying a property that does not need much work.

Care and Maintenance of Your Property

The condition and presentation of your property prior to being let will help to determine the rent as well as the type of tenant you are likely to attract. If the property is badly presented, it will be more difficult to attract a good tenant than if you make the effort to present the property well. However, this does not mean you should 'go to town' on the expense; there is no point investing in a fancy light fitting, for example, when a simple one will work as well. It won't add value to the property nor will it allow you to increase the rent; it is simply an unnecessary expense.

Your first consideration in caring for your property is that it should, above all, be clean and free from any safety hazards. You do not want to cause injury to tenants. Make sure that gas safety certificates are obtained for the property and that there are no faulty electrics. Also ensure that there are no sharp edges anywhere, or loose carpets that could be tripped over.

You might even consider asking for advice from your local Health & Safety department at the council. They may be round to advise you later otherwise, on the calling of an unhappy tenant! It is not unknown for tenants to use 'Health & Safety issues' as an excuse for not paying the rent: don't give them this excuse!

It is a legal requirement to equip rented properties with smoke alarms and these should be fitted as necessary and checked between tenancies. You should also advise tenants to check their fire alarms every three months.

Think of the security of the property, particularly when empty. Put lights on a timer device that goes on and off at different times to give the appearance of being occupied (or leave a landing or other light on). If necessary, close curtains in the lounge so that people cannot look into the property and see that it is empty. Are the windows lockable? This can be an insurance requirement too.

If the property is empty in winter, leave the heating on a low setting to avoid freezing pipes. Alternatively, you may choose to drain the water from pipes and tanks.

Fixtures and fittings for a rental property should always be of good hardwearing quality, as they will not have an easy life with tenants! Prices seem to vary greatly between suppliers and it is hard to beat places such as B&Q (www.diy.co.uk) or Screwfix (www.screwfix.co.uk) for quality and price. Dave has refitted a couple of our kitchens with very reasonably priced and attractive units from B&Q and he seems to make daily trips to Screwfix. We only refit kitchens that are in real need of it. Never go to any unnecessary expense. How do you know whether a new kitchen or bathroom is necessary? Dave's advice is: if in doubt, leave it out. Bear in mind that tenants often don't take care of things the way owners do. Make sure things are fitted very securely; perhaps use extra long screws when fitting a towel rail or toilet roll holder for example, which could get pulled off.

Gardens should be kept unfussy and easy for tenants to maintain. Rare is the tenant who is into gardening. You might provide tenants with a lawnmower in the hope they will mow the lawn but we find they are inclined to do so only when the grass is a foot high and end up breaking the mower! If you do give them a mower, make sure it is a Flymo as this has more chance of surviving use on very overgrown grass.

You will probably wonder whether you should furnish your property to let or not. We do not furnish our properties now as the tenants we get from the council are happy to take unfurnished. We used to provide kitchen appliances (or 'white goods') and allowed some flexibility on this, according to the response to advertising. Dave was particularly pleased not to supply washing machines any more, as it got to the point where he had 50 washing machines to manage and they need attention at surprising frequency!

Some tenants will have, or will be happy to purchase, their own kitchen appliances, while others may want them as well as beds and other things. Occasionally we used to extend to supplying beds in addition to the kitchen appliances. Beds and other soft furnishings must meet with fire safety standards and carry a fire safety certificate. We only supplied electric cookers (unless a gas cooker is already fitted) as gas cookers have to be serviced annually which costs money.

We have always bought second-hand appliances through free ads in the Friday-Ad local paper. By looking on their website instead of waiting for the paper to be published, we were always sure of getting what we were looking for. This is the cheapest way to buy appliances and we have found it entirely satisfactory as we can ask to see appliances working and often get the original receipt and service history, if any. We have an electrician friend who can check them over for us.

When installing a washing machine to an existing worktop arrangement, you may need to cut off a moulded plug and fit a new one to pass through the worktop to the socket.

Always try to buy things where possible from sales such as car boot sales, charity shops, garage sales, markets and auctions. Dave has bought sets of taps from car boot sales for only £1 whereas they start from about £20 in the shops.

Dave's Tip...

Along with a toolbox, Dave suggests keeping a supply of commonly needed maintenance items in the car to avoid extra trips to get them, including:

> Screws   > light bulbs
> mastic & gun   > inspection lamp
> extension lead   > carrier bags
> bin liners for rubbish removal   > 13 amp plugs
> riggers gloves   > knee pads   > tap washers
> fibre washers   > fuses   > fuse wires   > PTFE tape
> electrical screw connectors

More Tips from Dave

Don't bother to have curtains with pulleys, as tenants always manage to break these. When the pulley system breaks, you can put curtain rings around the rail and keep it.

Replace fluorescent lights with ordinary ones when they fail. With fluorescent lights, the tube is more difficult to change and you also need to replace the starter.

If you have a broken microwave or other medium sized item from a property, you can ask to throw it in the dustbin lorry instead of making an extra trip to the dump.

Do the rounds of properties when possible to avoid unnecessarily doubling up on trips, by arranging to do several maintenance jobs on the same day or evening; and collect rents too while you're there.

It is worth learning some basic plumbing skills as many maintenance problems that come up are basically plumbing matters, including:

- Dripping tap

- Toilet that won't flush

- Blocked toilet

- Leaking toilet

- Blocked sink

- Broken shower

- No hot water

If you need to improve your knowledge base, there are many good DIY books available and you can borrow from the library if you don't wish to buy. You could also enquire at your local adult education centre or technical college about short courses in plumbing and other skills.

If a sink is blocked, try to unblock it first simply by using a plunger. A concertina type one is better than a rubber cup type. If necessary, also try to put hot or boiling water and washing up liquid down the sink (works well for build-up of fat and grease). When a kitchen sink is blocked, the problem is usually fat, pasta or rice. As a last resort you may try a strong chemical such as Dam Buster, which is very strong (but don't get it on your clothes!) This should only be used after taking the pipework apart to drain off the water.

If a blockage goes deeply down in the pipes and cannot be reached, it may need to be cleared using a set of drain rods, which only cost about £20 and are a worthwhile investment as they can save you calling upon Dyno-rod or the likes, who will charge at least £150 to unblock the pipes.

Dripping or leaking taps often occur because tap washers wear out. Fixing this is a fairly simple job that anyone can do. Keep an assortment of washers in your toolbox.

Inside the toilet cistern and in the cold water tank there is a ballcock, the seals of which can perish and leak. These cost only 20p or so and can be easily replaced. If you called upon a plumber, he would probably replace the whole ballcock unnecessarily and charge you lots of money for this.

Remember that keeping the property clean and in good repair not only helps to attract and keep tenants, but also maintains the value of the property. We sometimes buy properties that have been tenanted and often have a certain neglected look. Why didn't the owner go to the trouble of re-decorating before putting the property on the market, so he could get thousands more for the place? It would be a good investment to do so.

Some landlords can be distressed sellers themselves, who have become too bored or perhaps upset by bad tenants to care any more. Don't let this be you a few years down the line. Be prepared for the long haul.

Painting

Painting will add immeasurably to the overall appearance of the property, both inside and out. But, more importantly, a paint job can increase the value tremendously. It is perhaps the most cost-effective improvement you can undertake: inexpensive and relatively easy.

Usually a simple decorative scheme is best, with magnolia for the walls and white gloss woodwork. When painting the walls of a furnished room, you can simply move the furniture to the middle of the room.

If there is wallpaper at present you can paint over it, as long as it is sound. This involves less work than removing the paper and bear in mind that the walls underneath may have flaws that would be exposed otherwise.

If you do need to get rid of wallpaper, a steam stripper is very useful. They cost from about £20 and can also be used to help defrost freezers and clean greasy kitchen floors and surfaces.

Using a roller is quicker than a brush. Use brushes only for edges and for gloss work.

If you are freshening up with a coat of paint in the same colour, one coat should be sufficient. For a change of colour, you will probably need two coats of paint. You must wait for the first coat of paint to be properly dry before applying the second coat.

Rollers and brushes can be kept in a plastic bag overnight between coats of emulsion paint to save rinsing them out. Brushes used for gloss work can also be kept overnight in water.

If tenants ask to paint we allow them. It shows that they want to settle in the property and take a pride in it (as well as saving you a paint job!)

Flooring

Before deciding to replace carpet, ask yourself if it could be cleaned rather than replaced. We often clean the carpets in between tenancies.

Carpet is often the cheapest and easiest answer for flooring. We normally choose a dark beige colour. We buy cheap carpet because we find tenants will stain it and burn it regardless; there's no point getting expensive carpet. We never use gripper-rods and underlay.

Laminate flooring is often popular with tenants. We tend to use it at properties that have perhaps proved hard to let (because of location, for example). Viewers cannot resist the laminate flooring so they are more likely to take the property on.

Lino tiles in kitchens are easier and cheaper to fit than a sheet of lino, but that can be preferable in bathrooms, which get very wet.

Dave's Tip...

REPLACING A FAULTY ELECTRIC SHOWER:

There are two common causes of failure of showers to work properly:

Either the heating element has burnt out, in which case you just get a cold shower all the time. In this case it is probably best to replace the whole shower. I would tend not to bother to contact the manufacturer to try and get spare parts as tenants do not want the time delay that would involve. Showers can cost as little as £40.

Or, the solenoid valve has stopped working. I prefer not to buy showers with a solenoid valve, as it is prone to break. Cheaper showers do not have this anyway. If there's no water coming through at all, it's symptomatic of a failed solenoid valve. Again, I would suggest replacing the whole shower.

When replacing a shower, shut off the water supply at the stopcock and turn off the electricity by taking out the appropriate fuse. Turn on a cold tap to release the water pressure before you begin the work.

Managing your own property can seem quite daunting when you are new to property investing. We ourselves employed a letting agent at first to deal with the tenant management side of things. This can be useful, as you can see first hand how professional letting agents deal with matters. You can pick up tips, which may help you to feel confident about going it alone later, as we did after our first tenant.

As we became more experienced, one of my brothers decided to invest in property in our locality and get us to manage the properties for him. Later, a second brother followed suit. They now have twenty properties between them, which we manage.

Whether you employ a letting agent or not, property management must be approached with a good understanding of the work that professional property managers undertake, in respect of both the care of the property and the tenants. You need to be fully aware of the relevant laws, the appropriate procedures and the relevant paperwork and records to be kept. Mistakes could not only be costly, but you might find yourself unwittingly on the wrong side of the law. The worst-case scenario would be if a tenant died because of the landlord's ignorance about the need for regular gas services.

Furthermore, if you are not fully conversant with the right way to do things, you could end up with a bad tenant that you cannot get rid of due to errors you made in the paperwork when you set up the tenancy, or because you did not give them notice in the legally correct way. (This is further discussed in the next chapter, on Managing Your Tenants).

Service Options of Letting Agents

Most agents operate on a 'no let, no fee' basis and do not always require you to enter a sole agency agreement such as estate agents often do. You could choose to instruct several agents to try and find you a tenant and then use whichever one gets a tenant that you are happy with first. Whether letting agents expect sole agency varies from one area to another, so you need to ask.

When considering agents to use, it is worth asking them questions such as:

- What are their professional affiliations? For example, ARLA is the Association of Residential Letting Agents (www.arla.co.uk). Some lenders may stipulate that agents should be members of such a body but this does not guarantee that the agent is superior to an independent.

- Is the agent properly insured? The company should be a member of the Client Money Protection scheme, which provides professional indemnity insurance. This safeguards both the landlord's rent and tenants' deposits should the management company run into difficulties or even go bust.

- Do they manage property exclusively? If you are using agents who are also estate agents, do they have the same expertise or focus on lettings as a dedicated letting agent?

- What's their policy on handling emergency repairs? They should keep you informed of any large or expensive repairs that may need doing. Landlords would normally have an agreement with the agent to be informed of any work that needs doing over a certain amount, say £200. Note that a letting agent is very likely to put a mark-up on fees for maintenance work so that they effectively get further commission there, if you allow them to arrange for maintenance.

- Ask agents what further charges they might make to landlords and tenants. Some charge both of them for things like inventories, the tenancy agreement and may charge a registration fee to would-be tenants too.

The decision whether to use an agent does not need to be all or nothing, as many agents offer different levels of service, such as:

Tenant Introduction Service

This is the least pricey option (may be 5% of the first six months' rent) for landlords who want help in finding tenants but who will subsequently be on hand to deal with them personally. This service should include:

- Conducting an initial assessment of the property's rental potential and rent achievable

- Advertising and marketing the property

- Conducting all viewings on the landlord's behalf

- Carrying out all reference checks on prospective tenants

- Preparation of the Tenancy Agreement

- Preparation of an inventory and schedule of condition of the property. You may elect to do this yourself, as it will otherwise cost extra

Letting and Rent Collection

Aimed at landlords who want help with finding a tenant as well as the support of the agent on an ongoing basis, but who are happy to liaise with the tenant directly on maintenance issues. Agents may charge around 10% for this service which should include, in addition to the services for introduction only:

- The serving of any relevant legal notices during the tenancy

- Rent receipt and remittance to the landlord's account

- Checking the tenant out at the end of the tenancy

- Arranging tenancy renewals and rent increases

- Collecting a deposit from the tenant (normally equivalent to one or one and a half months' rent) to cover damage or loss other than fair wear and tear and unpaid rent.

Letting and Full Property Management

A full management service is aimed at landlords who do not live locally to the property and simply do not want any involvement in the management and maintenance. The fee for full management could be up to 15% of the rent; bear in mind that does not include any maintenance that may need to be done!

This service should include, in addition to the letting and rent collection service:

- Regular visits by the agent to the property during the tenancy

- Liaising with tenants and maintenance contractors on maintenance issues

- Arranging estimates for works. Agents should use only qualified contractors and ensure that they are adequately insured

- Instructing and overseeing all repairs

- Arranging tenancy renewals and rent increases where appropriate

- Some letting agents may extend their services to property finding and the initial preparation of the property to let out. They may also offer insurances such as rental warranty insurance.

All this service sounds lovely, but remember that it all costs money. The more you depend on the services of others the higher the charges will be, eating into your profits. Whilst landlords may be wary of using letting agents because of the reduction in profits, we should remember on the other hand that agents deal with lettings every day and are very familiar with all the problems and pitfalls, so should be capable of dealing with crises calmly and effectively.

In spite of using an agent to manage our first tenancy, we did end up with a non-paying tenant who had to be got out. We learnt a lot and appreciated the support of the experienced letting agent throughout. However, we found out that using a letting agent cannot protect you from the fact that it is your problem when things go wrong: you are the one who will lose money and the problem is still yours ultimately!

Letting agents might not always live up to expectations and the following story illustrates a case where we were NOT happy with the advice or services of one agent.

Letting Agents – A Different Perspective

This is a true story, which illustrates the possible downside of using a letting agent instead of managing your own properties:

A few years ago, we had at one time four one bedroom flats available to let in the same town, as we had just bought two of them and two more had tenants move out.

Whilst we are normally happy to let and manage our own properties, having the four empty all at once caused concern and I contacted our local 'professional' letting agents. I invited the lady manageress of the agency to see our properties, with a view to her taking these on to her books and looking for tenants in tandem with our own attempts at advertising.

When she came to look at our flats, this letting agent went round each flat saying it needed refurbishing, or at least to be fully re-decorated, totally new flooring and in one case a new kitchen and bathroom too. I thanked her for the advice but said we felt the places were all adequate as they were and that we would not at the present time wish to do as she suggested. I was even more shocked when she replied that she simply would not take any of them on to her books in that case, as it meant more to her to maintain her reputation for only having 'smart' places on her books. She tried to justify this further by insisting that the agency only took on very professional tenants, whereas we would probably get a lower class of tenant.

I proceeded to advertise the properties privately and we had plenty of calls. All the properties were well thought of by our viewers and all let within a week or two. So we did not need the letting agency after all.

A while later, a flat in the same block as one of ours came up for sale and when it sold we heard it was to an investment buyer. Next thing we knew, there was a skip outside and out came the 'old' kitchen and bathroom. By and by, a sign went up outside 'flat to let' from the same letting agent that rejected ours. Since the flat is in our town, we drive by there regularly and saw that the agent's sign remained for months 'to let'. We looked in the local paper and found the rent being asked for the flat was £525 pcm. We let our flat out for £450 pcm, easily and quickly. I suppose they would need more for theirs, to cover the costs of the work done and now also the long void due to the rent being excessive! Eventually, we saw in the paper that the rent was now reduced to £495 pcm. It still took weeks, but finally a tenant moved in.

In this case the letting agent considered their own reputation more important than whether it was economic for us to carry out work which we did not consider necessary. The agent's financial gain was maximised by seeking to maximise the rent for the property, regardless of the length of the initial void, which did not affect them financially. However, the same simply does not apply to the landlord. Let's look at the figures, taking the above as an example:

Agent seeks: £525 pcm x 12 = £6,300 rent per annum

We seek: £450 pcm x 12 = £5,400 rent per annum

The agent seeks, over a year, to get £900 more rent than us.

In this example, what happened in fact was that our flat was empty for no more than one month, while the agency let flat was empty for five months, during which time the rent asked was revised downwards to £495 pcm.

So the actual rents gained over the course of a year, appear thus:

Agency let flat:

£495 x (12 - 5) = £3,465 rent per annum, less 15 % agency fees = **£2,945.25**

Our self managed flat: £450 x (12 - 1) = **£4,950.00** rent per annum

Therefore, the real outcome is that we got £2,004.75 more income. We could buy a new kitchen and bathroom with that! More importantly, though, the landlord using the agency would have **negative cash flow problems** for months assuming he had a mortgage to pay and that could wipe some investors out financially, leading to repossession or even bankruptcy! Don't take this lightly.

Recently, we heard that the man in the flat below the one let out by the agency is selling his, because he is fed up with the noisy and loutish behaviour of the tenants in the agency let flat. So their claim to attract better tenants was disproved also.

This is of course only an example of one agent I have come across. I know many property investors who have good agents that they are very happy with.

Planning of Works Prior to Letting

If work needs doing to let the property initially, it is best to line up quotes from tradesmen (if required) during the purchase period. Work out your budget and the plan of works to be done in terms of time required and the best order of works.

I include below an example of a budget and plan which we were asked to submit to our lender, for a property we wished to buy in September 2003. The surveyor had initially reported back to the mortgage company that he recommended not granting the buy to let mortgage on the property until we submitted this plan, which led to that decision been overturned in our favour.

A budget and plan of works for a repossessed house in need of refurbishment, as requested by our mortgage lender:

Statement and Schedule of Anticipated Works and Costs Involved

We currently own a total of 35 (at Oct 2003) buy-to-let properties (all fully tenanted), including 16 properties of the same type as the property in question, terraced houses built circa 1970 in the same neighbourhood. We have always, on the whole, bought properties that require some work to be presentable for letting, since such properties present a discount to the normally expected purchase cost. The current average cost for this type of property in this neighbourhood is £130,000 and this property, at £101,750, offers an incredible discount to this price.

Although ugly in the sense of needing cleaning, painting and new carpets throughout, as well as the garden being overgrown, we believe this property is fundamentally sound and this belief is based on the following evidence:

- It is a modern mid-terraced property (built about 1970) and we can see that:

- The properties to either side are well kept and sound;

- There is absolutely no evidence of subsidence, damp, woodworm or any other infestation;

- The roof and brickwork are sound;

- There is no internal damage at the property from fire, flood, or other hazard.

Furthermore, based on our experience of letting similar properties, it is our opinion that:

- The bathroom is in presentable condition and not in need of refurbishment;

- The kitchen is also acceptable and not in need to refurbishment either.

- The windows are acceptable and we would not anticipate replacing them.

- Although there is evidence that the property was not well lived in by the previous owner, it has been cleared out at least; which is better than some of our other properties, including our most recent purchase where we had to remove a lot of furniture and rubbish that was left as well as all flooring, and had to replace the kitchen.

Obviously, we appreciate that since this property is repossessed, the services have been disconnected and since we have been unable to test them, there is a risk of problems lurking. We have bought repossessed properties before, one of which was in an obviously worse state than this one, so we feel reasonably experienced in dealing with problems that may arise. On this point, we would like to say:

- Gas system: Bearing in mind the age of the property, we recognise there is always the risk of problems, mainly that a new boiler may be required. Even in pretty properties we have bought, the boiler has been "condemned" at times by our gas service contractor, the cost of replacement being £1,300 (replacement warm air system boiler).

- Electricity: There is no evidence of any particular problems, so again why should any be expected any more than at other properties? However, we are more than willing to factor in possible work required which should cost no more than £500.

- Plumbing: There is no sign of any internal water damage at the property caused by leaky plumbing. At a repossessed property we bought a couple of years ago, there were signs of water damage and when the water was turned on it did indeed leak; we paid a plumber about £200 to trace and fix the leak. This is something we could cope with if necessary, but we do not anticipate having this problem.

- Woodwork: Again, at the repossessed property mentioned above, the floorboards in the bathroom needed replacing by a carpenter due to the previous plumbing problems, which cost only about £50. Again, we do not anticipate any need for this, but feel we could cope with the situation if required.

- Drains: We did have problems at the above property with blocked drains, which involved calling out "Drain Doctor" for a cost of £200. So be it.

Summary Schedule of Work and Possible Expenses:

PAINTING AND DECORATING THROUGHOUT:

Time required: 2 weeks Cost: £200 maximum (We do most of this ourselves; may use hired labour at £50 per room for max 3 rooms)

NEW CARPETS/FLOORING THROUGHOUT:

Time required: 1 week Cost: £300 (We fit ourselves)

CLEARING THE GARDEN:

Time required: 1 week Cost: £0 (We do ourselves, taking excess plant material to the dump in our cars)

ANY OTHER MATTERS (SUCH AS SERVICES REQUIRING REPAIRS):

Time required: max 6 weeks Cost: £2,250 (Based on the total of possible expenses for services as discussed above)

Total Time Required and Expenses as Outlined Above:

Maximum time until let out: 6 to 8 weeks

We anticipate being able to advertise the property to let just 2 or 3 weeks after purchase, by which time prospective tenants will be able to appreciate the work in progress and it will take time to check out their references and for them to give notice at their current place. This is how we proceeded at the other repossessed property we bought which was in worse condition and we found this worked very well.

Maximum anticipated costs: £3,000

This figure is based on the £2,250 for service repairs, plus £200 for decorating, £300 for carpets and allowing an extra £250 for miscellaneous expenses.

We would be happy to accept that you [the lender] may wish to make a retention on the mortgage of about £3,000 pending work to be done.

In conclusion, we believe that at a cost of £101,750 this property, which is basically sound and of a type we are well familiar with (already owning 16 of them), offers an incredible discount to the average cost of £130,000 for this type of property.

We are most anxious to move forward with the purchase as soon as possible. The mortgagees in possession have already requested exchange of contracts by 10th September, and we are concerned that the property may be more fully marketed and the price bid higher if we do not move quickly.

We would appreciate a swift and positive response from you. If there were any specific areas of concern to the valuer that we have not mentioned above, we would welcome the opportunity to address these matters.

Yours sincerely

Mr David Bryant & Mrs Angela Bryant

After considering our plan of works, the mortgage lender over-ruled the surveyor's recommendation and granted us the mortgage on the property (with a retention of £3,000 as I suggested).

We bought the property and found all the services were fine. We spent a lot less on the property than the £3,000 we budgeted for and the property was easily let, as it sparkled with fresh magnolia paint and wooden flooring by the time tenants saw it!

Weighing Up the Decision to Quit Work

Financially, the decision to do your own maintenance has to be weighed up against other considerations such as how much you earn or can make doing other things. If doing your own maintenance means you have to give up your day job at some point when you have a growing number of properties, is the loss of primary income justified by the increase in profit? If you earn more than the average wage or have only a few properties, it may not worth giving up work only to undertake property maintenance.

Of course, you will take into account other considerations such as whether by giving up your job you would also be likely to take on other business arrangements that could enhance your income further. You may wish to give up work to concentrate full-time on property development, or sourcing and buying below market value deals. I know people who have made a great success of this.

If you do manage your own properties, related self-employment might be a good alternative to a job, such as becoming a qualified gas fitter; doing handyman work for others; doing refurbishment work for yourself and others; becoming a letting agent; or offering bridging finance. You may wish to start up an unrelated business, but beware of spreading your attention too thinly. Focus is a fundamental principle of success in business.

Whatever choices you make will have varying effects on your own lifestyle. The greater your personal involvement with your properties, the greater the impact these will have on your lifestyle.

Some people may own vast portfolios which are totally managed by others and affect their personal lifestyle little. However, the size of the portfolio is no guarantee of anything; I know of some people with big portfolios they don't self-manage who have gone bankrupt.

We ourselves have chosen to do much of the work and thus, for us, owning buy to let properties has become a way of life and our business. Since Dave gave up his day job, he has taken over more of the work that I used to help with while he was still working, so that I now get to concentrate on other things. For Dave, property maintenance and tenant management is quite a job, now that he has our sixty plus properties to manage and another twenty five for my brothers.

As Dave's Diary shows, hardly a day goes by without some property problem that needs to be dealt with. Both tenant and maintenance-related problems arise regularly. Dave enjoys the work on the whole, as it suits his character to do practical work of this nature. He enjoys the freedom from the former office-based employment and feels closer to the children and me as he is around more of the time.

Dave will always deal with tenants' problems promptly. One advantage we have over any letting agent is that we are always available for our tenants, at all times of day and night, 365 days a year - and tenants do like to phone at odd hours with emergencies or even on Christmas Day (which they may not celebrate themselves). We could make ourselves unavailable at times, but we find the level of our tenants' demands is fine and we are glad to know tenants are happy with the service they get from us. Dave will always answer the phone, but may say he'll go round tomorrow if a tenant phones on Christmas Day!

Developing the Infrastructure for Maintenance Work

If you are prepared to do maintenance for your properties, it is worth thinking about whether you have the infrastructure to do so. There is more to it than simply having a good set of tools, though that is a good starting point!

Dave's Tip...

 I have an estate car which is brilliant for delivering furniture and kitchen appliances (as well as a sack barrow). The car is also suitable for garden trimmings and for taking rubbish to the dump. It is used as a van with tools and general decorating materials much of the time. But it can also be used for the family when required.

We have a workshop in addition to our garage, which is used for storing spare appliances, as well as carpeting, decorating and maintenance materials. We bought the workshop when we started to acquire more properties, and put the cost down as a business expense.

Using the Services of Others

No matter how handy you are or how well kitted out, there are bound to be times when you need extra help from tradesmen. The main people that we use regularly are:

CORGI registered gas fitter: You must arrange for the property to have any gas systems (normally the central heating) and appliances that you supply tested by a CORGI registered engineer and obtain a landlord's gas safety certificate, prior to letting. A copy of the certificate should be kept at the property for the tenants. If there is any question of electrical problems the electrics should also be tested.

We have a great, independent gas service engineer whose charges are reasonable and who can do the work required promptly. We had some trial and error before finding someone we were happy with and I think this is inevitable. It seems to us that small is beautiful with gas fitters; big firms may not be interested - especially in a landlord with few properties - or they may treat you as second rate (as well as charging more); some only do work for local councils or other big operators.

Electrician: There is no annual inspection required for the electrics in the same way as for gas, but it is nevertheless imperative that you employ the services of a qualified electrician if there is any question as to the safety of the property's electrical system or of any electrical items supplied.

Carpenters: Again, a small operator will tend to charge less and keep it simple, in our experience. For example, we had an old wooden porch at a property and wanted a simple solution to improve the look of it. Several carpenters refused to do what we suggested, which was simply replacing a few bits of wood. We found a humble carpenter who did what we asked and the result was perfectly satisfactory.

To sum up then, there are a lot of pros and cons to weigh up when considering whether to do your own management and property maintenance and this is bound to be unique for each person in some ways. There can be an element of trial and error. The easiest or most convenient option will often be the most expensive. Remember to weigh up the various choices in financial or cost effective terms rather than simply choosing the easiest option. In this way, you will eventually find the best solution for you.

Whether you feel that doing your own property management is for you or not, there is no doubt it increases profits as well as your control over the business. It allows you to develop a solid business model that works.

So now you should be ready for Managing Your Tenants.

Chapter 8

Managing Your Tenants

"As far as possible, without surrender, be on good terms with all persons. Speak your truth quietly and clearly; and listen to others."
Excerpt from Desiderata, by Max Erhmann

In this chapter I will look at:

- What it takes to be a landlord who manages his own tenants

- Advertising and attracting tenants

- Having viewers - who to expect and how to proceed

- Should you take DSS?

- Checking out references

- Types of tenancy and tenancy agreements

- Tenants - what are they like?

- When the rent is late

- Taking legal action when necessary

The question of whether to manage your own tenants touches most closely on a need to examine your own personality and abilities. So the question you need to answer is:

Should I become a landlord who manages my own properties?

I think the qualities that are important for you to have as a landlord if you are to manage your own properties, include:

- A certain ability to remain calm, rational and slightly detached when dealing with tenants and viewers

- An ability to treat tenants fairly and with consideration without getting personally friendly

- Being contactable and able to see to problems and maintenance issues promptly

Dave is very well suited to being a landlord as he has the above qualities and is also very reliable, committed, honest and trustworthy.

Excerpt from Dave's Diary...

Tuesday 9th March, 2004:
I had a viewer at 7 pm and one at 9 pm at 5K. I also went to have a look at 26S boiler again, which was losing pressure, so I went to check that and I bled all the radiators. Then I went to 5R and 7M to collect Letsure forms that had been returned there.

I admit to not having the natural qualities that are required to deal well with tenants, and this became apparent in the early days when I tried to help with property viewers and tenants. Problems arose as people would take one look at me and start asking for concessions and things, as I am 'too soft' according to Dave, who soon suggested that I leave the tenant management to him.

Lodgers as a training ground

In our own case, Dave's future ability to deal with tenants was given a training opportunity during our earlier years when we had lodgers. I am not suggesting that taking lodgers is a necessary precursor to becoming a landlord, only that for us it revealed the dynamics of the landlord/tenant relationship, and also revealed Dave's ability to manage that relationship well. In particular, he is very resilient to attempts at emotional manipulation. He also has a very straightforward sense of right and wrong: it is right for lodgers and tenants to pay their rent and wrong not to – if they behave in a wrong way, in this or any other respect, they have to leave. Simple.

By the way, if you are experiencing financial struggles at this stage and particularly if you have set up home but have no children, taking lodgers can be a very good idea. The income is tax free up to £4,250 pa under the Government's Rent-a-Room scheme, introduced to encourage people to rent out a room in their house. This income can, as it did for us (and for which we are ever grateful), make the difference between only just making ends meet financially and actually being able to save some money, sowing the seeds for your bright financial future.

By taking a lodger, you are offering cheap accommodation in a welcome homely environment. Some of our lodgers over the years became good friends. You soon get to know people when they are living in your home and you can afford to relax into friendliness with those who prove to be of good, honest character. However, it is important to remember that the basis of the relationship is a business one.

If you do have the opportunity to take lodgers, it will certainly add to your confidence about becoming a landlord when you buy your first investment property and are ready to get tenants.

Keeping it local

If you wish to manage your property yourself, I advise you to think very carefully before buying non-local. Based on my investing experience, I am glad that I did not choose to invest in properties further than 5-10 miles away. It can be tempting to buy properties in a town further afield, where the gross yield may be greater than more locally, and I gave this matter serious consideration in the early days. However, when call-outs to a growing number of properties started piling up, we realised it was a must for Dave not to have too far to travel.

I have heard of young single landlords, in particular, who approach their investment properties with the view: "I don't want to put all my eggs in one basket by having properties just in one or two local towns. Besides, I have plenty of time and enjoy long car journeys, so it is fine for me to get five properties in towns up to a 3 hour drive away each in different directions." That approach may be fine for you now. But have you looked ahead in life and considered whether this will be a satisfactory situation when you have a wife and children?

Excerpt from Dave's Diary...

Friday 19th March, 2004:
4 o'clock at 5R: Moved the guys in, took their money and gave them the keys. Then at 7 o'clock got a call from 130S saying could I take these mattresses and the sofa away, because they've bought a sofa bed. So I went and did that. Then at 9 pm, got a call from 5K - they had locked themselves out, so I had to go round there and let them in.

Buy to let is best thought of as a medium to long-term investment, so you should try to anticipate your likely future circumstances and not just your present situation.

Setting the Rent

Before advertising your property for rent, you need to establish what rent you can get for the property by investigating the going rate for similar properties in the area. Keep an eye on rents being achieved over a few weeks before deciding and always keep your knowledge up-to-date when your property becomes re-available at the end of a tenancy.

Thorough research to find the average rent includes:

- **Property Websites:** Sites such as rightmove (would you like to change to hyperlink?) provide a great way of finding information fast and comparing similar properties in an area.

- **Local papers:** By looking in local papers, you can find properties to let, not only with agents but also privately advertised.

- **Local agents:** Ask as a prospective landlord client, or even as a prospective tenant, about rental prices and demand for rental property in the area.

When comparing your property with similar ones, note the following factors:

- **The location** - find comparables in the exact same neighbourhood, which makes all the difference.

- **The size of the property** - including number of rooms - reception and bedrooms (note whether double or single), downstairs or separate wc, garden or garage and parking available.

- **The quality of the property condition** - double glazing, central heating, decorative order.

- Quality of the kitchen and bathroom, fixtures and fittings.

- Whether it is furnished, unfurnished or part furnished.

How to Get Tenants

As we manage our properties ourselves, we have always tended to attract tenants who shy away from letting agents for various reasons; they feel more comfortable dealing with us and often recommend us to friends. We have built up quite a network of tenant contacts and have a waiting list for our properties.

A few of our properties are leased to a Housing Association (which I discuss more in a later section of this chapter). We responded to a plea they made in an article in the local paper, when they were looking for more accommodation. Keep an eye on the local papers when you have property to let, as you never know what relevant piece of information you may find.

A couple of years ago, when we were advertising a property to rent in the local paper, a woman from the local council phoned us. She explained that she had just been employed in a new role of Housing Officer with responsibility for finding private accommodation for tenants who approached the council and whom they could not house themselves due to the shortage of council houses. There is a big demand and we now get most of our new tenants this way. If you are prepared to take so-called 'DSS tenants', ask about this at your local council.

Of course, unless or until you get to this position, there will be times you need to do some…

Advertising

How should you go about advertising? It is important to establish the best advertising media for your type of property and location. You can advertise your property on the internet, at sites such as www.torent.co.uk for free. You may also like to consider advertising in a specialist rental publication.

It is worthwhile trying a dummy run of advertising before a property is even purchased, both to test the tenant demand and the effectiveness of the advertising media.

In my experience of investing in my own and a neighbouring town, I have found that a fairly simple advert in the local paper works best. In my own town, I only have one-bed flats and these are always very well sought after. I live in a small town where there is no excessive competition from other landlords. A simple lineage ad in the local paper does the trick.

In our larger, neighbouring town, demand for rental property is still healthy, but it is worth paying a little extra for a 'box' advert just to make ours stand out. The cost for the box advert is £16.95 per week (for two papers) as opposed to £9.50 for a lineage ad. It is always wise to get a copy of the paper yourself and to check that the advert is in as it should be. Mistakes can be made at newspapers, as I have found a few times. At least if you phone to point out that your advert did not go into the paper as planned, you will be entitled to the following week's advertising free of charge!

When considering the wording for your advertisement, do note whether adverts are listed alphabetically. A simple change of wording from 'House to let' to 'A house to let' can bring an improved response to your advertisement.

Advertisement Respondents - Dealing with Enquiries

I suggest that you keep a list of questions by the phone as prompts to your memory. When you chat with enquirers, let the conversation flow as naturally as possible.

Your note of questions to ask callers might include:

- "Where are you living at the moment?"

- "Why are you moving from there?"

- "Where do you work?"

- "What work do you do then?"

- "How old are you?"

- "Do you have a current or previous landlord?"

If the caller's profile is not within the type of tenants you take, it will save time if you tell the person you are sorry and perhaps explain that your insurance company or lender does not permit that category of tenant.

If an applicant does seem suitable and he/she is interested in viewing the property, you can arrange for them to view. At this point, be prepared to:

- Give them the address and directions of how to get there

- Tell them how to get there by public transport, if necessary

- Take a contact telephone number for them - you may need to let them know if you will have a problem keeping to the appointed time. If they are arranging to view a few days hence you may like to phone and check they are still coming shortly before the appointment

- Tell them about the local facilities, schools, etc.

- Tell them what furniture if any is at the property and if you are flexible about what you will provide

- Let them know what the procedure will be, if they want to rent the property after viewing it, and in particular if you will require a holding deposit

It is a good idea to arrange viewings at half-hourly intervals, or even double up appointments if there is a good response, as it will save you re-visiting the property on too many separate occasions.

Viewers

When you meet viewers, as well as showing them the property and pointing out its merits, you will need to answer any questions they have about the property and the area. If they are interested in going ahead with renting the property, you will also need to explain to them the process involved, including filling out the paperwork. The paperwork includes reference checking forms and the assured shorthold tenancy agreement, both of which are discussed further below.

Viewers may also request a standing order mandate for paying the rent, so you should keep these handy. We are flexible with tenants about how they wish to pay the rent each month, whether by standing order, cheque in the post, or payment into my account. Some tenants even prefer us to collect cash, and although this is not our preference, we like to be flexible.

What type of viewers can you expect?

According to a recent survey, the typical tenant turns out to be:

- Male (60%)

- Under 30 years old (71%)

- Single (51%)

- With no children (78%)

- Has rented before (69%)

- Intends to continue renting for at least another year (70%)

- Rents because he cannot afford to buy his own property (42%)

You must be prepared for all-comers when you go to meet viewers. You may even meet people who feel desperate when they need a home and possibly cannot afford to buy. It is important not to be narrow-minded or prejudiced when dealing with prospective tenants.

The type of tenant you are likely to get depends on the type of property and the area in which you buy. As I live near a major airport that is a large employer, it is likely that I will get applicants who work at the airport. Because I specialise in the lower end of the market, I am more likely to attract baggage handlers than aircrew.

The more professional tenants generally will be choosy about which property they rent and will seek to live in the more expensive parts of town. They will expect the best fixtures and fittings, and high quality appliances; often they will seek a place to rent through a letting agent.

If you like the idea of renting to families you should remember that they will often be looking for a house with a garden. Some families who are seeking to rent privately will also be recipients of benefits.

DSS and LHA (Local Housing Allowance)

If you want to consider renting to DSS or benefit claimants, you must check first that this will be OK with your lender and your insurance company. The money can be paid direct to you from the council depending on circumstances, or to the tenant by default since the rules changed. The advantage of arranging for benefits to be paid to you as landlord is that you are sure to get the money. If the money goes to the tenant initially, you are relying on them to pass it on to you. On the other hand, if money is paid directly to you and it is subsequently found that the tenant was making a false claim, the money could be reclaimed from you.

People sometimes phone up and ask if you will take DSS tenants, but it is important you make sure they will actually be eligible for benefits. You could ask if they have a history of DSS they can prove, or have evidence of initial enquiries being positively received by the council. (They can normally request a 'pre-determination'). Ask whether they will be eligible for enough benefit to cover the full amount of the rent (usually not) and how they feel about making up the difference. When they move in, can they cover the deposit and first month's rent? Can they pay the rent if necessary until their benefits claim is processed? The time taken for claims to be processed varies and can be quite long. As a landlord you must be prepared for this delay.

The system for benefits in respect of housing has changed as from April 2008 and the old Housing Benefit has been replaced by the Local Housing Allowance (LHA). We have found the new LHA rates to be very favourable for our properties as have many investors I know throughout the UK, so do consider taking on tenants eligible for this. Details of the new LHA rates in your area may be available on your local council's website, or visit the LHA Direct website at:

https://lha-direct.therentservice.gov.uk

It must be noted that benefits will be paid in arrears by the council and can be subject to revision if the tenant's circumstances change. Since April 2007 benefits do normally go direct to tenants rather than to the landlord, although they can be given direct to the landlord following arrears of two months or more, as well as if the tenant is deemed to be 'vulnerable'.

Be cosmopolitan

Our local airport economy makes the area very cosmopolitan. Indeed, the country as a whole is increasingly multi-cultural. In our area it is the young, foreign contract workers who are the main body of workers in need of private landlord accommodation. In general they tend to avoid the high street letting agents because they are constantly turned away. Some enquirers have a poor command of English or a foreign accent that is difficult to understand. When differences of culture and values are added to the equation, it can be hard to have a conversation with such enquirers. It is very important to have patience and respect for all callers who may become your tenants and as such will be the life-blood of your business.

If you live or invest in a town where there is a university or large college, you should expect to get students as tenants. Any major organisation or employer will have a bearing on the type of tenants you are likely to get.

Check references and choose your tenants

Collect personal information from viewers who are interested in the property. Be prepared with a form for them to complete either on the spot or to post back to you, requesting their personal details. The following should be obtained in order for you to initiate referencing, preferably via a tenant vetting agency such as www. letsure.co.uk, which supplies a form for collecting details they will check. Note that you will not be able to request bank references personally. Details requested should include:

- Full name and date of birth

- Current address and previous address (if less than 3 years)

- Occupation, time at company, address of employer (for reference)

- Need to acquire Housing Benefit for rental payment?

- Name, role, address, telephone of guarantor (if applicable)

- Children, pets, smoker preferences

- Next of kin/emergency contact telephone number

- Name and address of character referee

- Banking details - sort code, account number, branch address (only an agency such as Letsure can follow up)

- You may ask for their National Insurance number

If you have several people interested in the property, your decision will be based on various factors including, in addition to the above:

- Whether they seem honest and good

- Whether they have a good, traceable work and previous landlord history (as verified by Letsure or other tenant referencing agency)

- Whether they seem well able to afford the full deposit and rent

- Whether, if it is a group of people, the group appears stable and close-knit

- Whether they would appear to make good neighbours and fit in well in the area

Some people will say they want the property and take forms to fill in, but then not come back to you after all. Others do come back, but with incomplete information. You should always make it clear to people that you will continue to show the property to others until someone gives you a holding deposit and a properly completed form and you have agreed they seem a likely candidate. Even at this stage, they must understand that it is not a foregone conclusion that you will be taking them on as tenants until after their references have been checked.

You should request a holding deposit (say £200) from prospective tenants, for you to stop showing the property to further viewers. This will only be when you have agreed to consider them on the basis of your meetings and when they have satisfactorily completed tenant-referencing forms.

You will also want to choose tenants that wish to move in as soon as possible and who do not make too many demands for furniture and fixings! You may also consider their basic ability to cope with their own minor DIY emergencies, such as the pilot light going out on the boiler!

Types Of Lets

There are alternative types of agreement to the usual assured shorthold tenancy and it may be worth considering whether any of these may be suitable for your property circumstances.

Short Term Lets

These are especially suitable for contractors and often arranged by corporate bodies on behalf of their employees, usually through letting agents. Contractors need flexibility and their companies will expect to pay above average rents for short lets (cheaper than the alternative of paying for hotel accommodation). They will also require above average properties.

Holiday Lets

If you are purchasing a property for holiday lets in the UK you will need your visiting holidaymakers to sign and return before their stay, the 'booking terms and conditions' which effectively form a type of tenancy agreement. You will also need to obtain a booking deposit, which becomes non-refundable in the event of late cancellation of the holiday. Unlike most let property, the landlord is legally responsible for the council tax on holiday lets and will pay all utility bills; these will of course be reflected in your costs.

Leasing to a Housing Association

One alternative way of letting out your property is to lease it to a housing association. Housing associations work with the local council to alleviate the pressure on councils to provide housing for those on the council's housing waiting list.

We lease four of our properties to a housing association and are generally happy with the arrangement. It does reduce the ongoing workload of dealing with tenants and maintenance work. The main reasons we haven't leased more of our properties to the housing association are threefold:

- They only require two bedroom flats currently in our area

- Some of our flats were already occupied with long-standing tenants when we became aware of the opportunity

- Some of our flats (depending on the part of town where they are, mainly) attract higher rents than the housing association pay, which is a flat rate according simply to the number of bedrooms the property has, regardless of the location, size or quality of the particular property.

Here is an ex-council flat that we let to a housing association

Often, as in our case, the arrangement the housing association will have with landlords is to lease the property for an agreed five-year period. During this time (commencing with the first tenancy start date) landlords are guaranteed no voids and the housing association will accept responsibility for maintaining the property and returning it in the condition given. We are still responsible for major external maintenance work, such as a new roof (if it blows off!)

Leasing to a housing association has several advantages:

- Guarantee of no voids for five years (period may vary)

- Not having to deal directly with tenants

- Not having to worry about non-payment of rent

- Being able to satisfy the high demand from DSS claimants without the uncertainty that can accompany this. (You must make sure that it is acceptable to your lender and insurance company to do this).

To find out if there are any housing associations actively working in partnership with landlords in your area, contact your local council housing department. As mentioned earlier, we also get tenant referrals now from the council who are not in the housing association lease scheme.

HMO Lets

Houses in Multiple Occupation have been further discussed in Choosing Your Property. Remember that you must seek the approval of your lender and insurance company before considering this form of letting.

If you let out your property to separate individuals by the room, each tenant should have a separate AST agreement. It is worth noting that if you wish to let a property to a non-family group, you can have all tenants sign the same AST and recognise their joint and several responsibility as members of the group.

Any property with two or more unrelated persons is strictly defined as a HMO, but licensing will only be required (normally) for properties which are three or more storeys high with five or more persons.

Assured Shorthold Tenancy Agreements

The usual form of tenancy agreement is the assured shorthold, or short assured tenancy in Scotland. The AST protects the rights of the tenant and provides the framework for the landlord to effect an eviction if necessary.

The contract term should be for a 'fixed period' of a minimum six months, with a two-month period of notice required to regain possession. The six month tenancy gives the tenant some security of tenure and cannot be terminated except for non-payment of rent or other breach of the contract.

At the end of the six months, the tenancy may revert to a contractual periodic tenancy, running from one rent day to the next. This makes it easier for the landlord to regain possession quickly if necessary, as two months' notice may be given to tenants to leave just because the landlord wants to take back possession.

When suitable tenants have been found and the time arrives for them to move in, you will meet, normally at the property, to issue them with an assured shorthold tenancy agreement.

You should have a clause in the AST stating your entitlement to increase the rent periodically. If you are letting to sharers, you need to make sure a clause is added making each individual jointly named responsible for the rental commitment (a 'joint tenancy'), so that if one person leaves, the remaining sharers are responsible for all the rent.

Whether you are using a letting agent or managing the property yourself, do make sure the AST meets your requirements as the landlord, for example with regard to pets, children, smoking and allowing you reasonable access. I supply an assured shorthold tenancy agreement, as do most landlord organisations, so it is normally not necessary to involve a solicitor. You can adapt a given AST to suit your own circumstances by changing some of the clauses.

Don't forget to prepare an inventory of any appliances or furniture, as well as fixtures and fittings and general condition of the property and get the tenant to sign this too. Always get the tenant (or tenants) to sign the AST before you hand over the keys, as well as the full deposit (as discussed in the next section) and the first month's rent in cash. Always keep a full set of keys yourself for each property as well.

Two copies of the agreement should be prepared and both signed by the tenant. You keep the original and give your tenant the counterpart. You should also get a witness to the tenant's signature.

Always log the meter readings for gas and electricity when the tenants move in. We contact the utility companies ourselves with these readings, as well as the council for the council tax, and give the incoming tenants' names. It will help your tenants if you can provide them with contact details for the gas, electricity, water, telephone and council tax.

When you book tenants into the property, remember to show them how things work such as the boiler pilot, any alarms and other things which could help to avoid unnecessary call-outs. They will also appreciate any local information you can supply such as bus or train timetables.

Taking a Deposit

It is wise to always take a deposit from incoming tenants at the commencement of a tenancy, as this provides a buffer against non-payment of rent or disrepair which may have to be funded from the deposit, either during or at the end of the tenancy. A deposit is typically equivalent to 4–6 weeks' rent, normally less for small flats and more for bigger houses.

Any deposits taken since new regulations came into force in April 2007 must in some form be protected under a government approved tenancy deposit protection scheme. This may be on either a custodial or insurance-backed basis. The three providers of the schemes are:

The Deposit Protection Service (The DPS): This is the only custodial deposit protection scheme, is free to use and open to all Landlords and Letting Agents. The service is funded entirely from the interest earned from deposits held. Landlords and Letting Agents can register and make transactions online.

Tenancy Deposit Solutions Ltd (TDSL): This is a partnership between the National Landlords Association and an insurance company. This insurance-based tenancy deposit protection scheme enables landlords, either directly or through agents, to hold deposits.

The Tenancy Deposit Scheme (TDS): An insurance-backed deposit protection and dispute resolution scheme run by The Dispute Service that builds on a scheme established in 2003 to provide dispute resolution and complaints handling for the lettings industry. The new scheme enables letting agents and landlords to hold deposits.

Further details and contact for any of these schemes can be found at the government's informative website www.direct.gov.uk.

Energy Performance Certificates

Under new EU legislation, for any new tenancies commencing after 1st October 2008 you will need to provide an Energy Performance Certificate to prospective tenants. There is no need to obtain a certificate for an existing tenancy. Once obtained, a certificate remains valid for up to 10 years.

ERP inspections will need to be carried out by qualified inspectors and this service should be widely available from agents, surveyors and others (costs ranging from around £70 - £140 per property). The rented accommodation energy certificate consists of two ratings:

The SAP Rating:

This rating provides an indication of a property's energy efficiency. In basic terms this consists of insulation values, heating, and heat loss area. The higher the SAP rating, the lower the fuel costs to heat the home.

The Environmental Rating:

Is an assessment of the property's impact on the environment, with a computation on how much CO_2 (carbon dioxide) the property would produce on average in a year. The lower the rating the more impact it has on the environment.

How can you improve the Energy (SAP) rating?

The energy inspector will be able to provide some recommendations that can help to improve the ratings given in the certificate, if you so wish. These recommendations will vary depending on the house construction and type of heating employed in the home and they are of course aimed at reducing emissions and improving energy efficiency.

So you have tenants! What can you expect?

Dave deals with maintenance problems at our properties quickly and he takes this responsibility very seriously. Dave's motto on the business card that he hands out to tenants says: "Always there for you." However, the sentiment expressed can wear a bit thin at times!

Frequently tenants will move in to a property and then phone after a week or two to say: "The boiler is broken. There is no hot water." Dave has to go round, only to find they have unwittingly switched off the boiler (ditto the power shower…!) How to open the patio doors is another of life's great mysteries for some; or how to change a light bulb. Dave now carries spare light bulbs in the car. Often, when he is called to deal with any problem at a property, one or more rooms are in the dark because the light bulb has gone and the tenant is not capable of changing a bulb.

At times like this, which happen all too frequently, I wonder how landlords manage when they do not maintain their own properties. If a tradesman were called out, it would no doubt incur a service charge, not to mention that the tradesman may discover more imaginary faults.

A good low maintenance tenant is one that has some common sense around the house and can figure out or tackle little problems for themselves instead of calling the landlord out at the drop of a hat! A few simple questions about the prospective tenant's DIY abilities may well save you several unnecessary callouts.

Par for the Course

Once tenants have moved in to a property, as the landlord you have a duty to allow them 'quiet enjoyment' of the property. This is good for you, too, up to a point. When I think back to my days with lodgers I would cook for them, help with their washing and clean up after them. I even used to make their beds in the early days. At least with tenants, they do not expect you to do those things. The downside is that as a landlord you are not privy to what they get up to - and tenants get up to EVERYTHING!

We have come to take some of the relatively minor offences by tenants in our stride. After all, with this number of properties, we are housing well over 100 people and that is a lot to keep an eye on. We make sure the properties are safe and in a fit state of repair, always have the annual gas safety checks done, ensure that the electricity is safe and that smoke alarms are fitted and working.

Beyond that we try to leave the tenants to their 'quiet enjoyment'. Tenants will do things they shouldn't and often we just accept that we will clean the place up when they move out and, if appropriate and possible at that time, will withhold any necessary money from the deposit.

So what should you expect tenants may get up to?

- They smoke

- They drink (and spill it all over the carpets)

- They repaint rooms in unusual colours

- They take down our curtains and lose them

- They scuff up the paintwork

- They NEVER clean the oven

- All tenants leave at least one trademark iron-shaped burn in the carpet

- They allow the place to get dirty and smelly

- They have friends staying that they shouldn't

- They end relationships and start new ones, leading to confusion

- They make noise that disturbs the neighbours

- They drive across grass verges

- They NEVER mow the lawn

- They leave unwanted furniture and appliances in the garden

- They forget to put rubbish out for so long the dustbin men won't take it when they suddenly leave ten unsecured bin bags outside

- They NEVER clean the kitchen or bathroom

- They may get a pet without asking

- They forget when it's rent day until reminded

- They are broke, in spite of having flashy mobile phones, televisions and hi-fis

- They don't pay their other bills

If you find all this too shocking then:

1.   You may drive yourself up the wall

2.   It may be better not to have tenants!

Though probably not the answer, with around £45,000 of mortgage payments to make every year!

Added to the above, every possible life event will sooner or later befall some or other tenant. One of the privileges of having so many properties is that it can feel like we have somehow created a 'microcosm' of life; a whole little world, reflecting the world at large in some small, sometimes wondrous way!

Events that have befallen our tenants include:

- New babies being born

- Tenants getting married

- Tenants getting divorced

- Tenants losing their job

- Tenants going onto housing benefit

- Tenants being no longer eligible for benefits

- A tenant who died (a young man)

- A tenant who disappeared without trace

- Tenants who went to prison

- A stabbing of one tenant by another

- Tenants who threaten Dave

- Tenants who send us Christmas cards

Love 'em or not, that's tenants for you!

I would like to say that 95% of our tenants are very nice people, 95% of the time!

It has to be said that many tenants are fairly young, single folk who have not yet reached a stage in life where they want to settle down. It should come as no surprise therefore, that they might have more colourful lives than some of us landlords.

When to make Tenant Behaviour Your Business

The main circumstances of direct concern to the landlord are outlined below. When tenants:

- Have the neighbours complaining

- Don't pay the rent, even when prompted

- May be involved in all sorts of criminal activity and the police phone you

- Have become abusive or violent (police assistance should be sought)

- Are causing safety hazards in the property

This is when I am glad of my big, brave husband and why managing your own property is not for the faint hearted.

Dealing with Complaints by Neighbours

Dealing with complaints by neighbours in an appropriate manner can be tricky to handle well. Here are some of the complaints of varying seriousness that we've had from neighbours about our tenants:

- They never mow the lawn

- They let the dandelions grow

- They take the wrong parking space (even though there are no allocated spaces)

- Their kids kick balls about the green

- They are rude

- They exhibit drunken behaviour

- They have loud, wild parties (and didn't invite us!)

- They bring home shopping trolleys

- They don't bag up their rubbish properly

- They look aggressive

- They lower the tone of the neighbourhood

  And:

- Neighbours want Dave to phone the police about the disturbance

- Neighbours want Dave to evict the tenants immediately for even the slightest misdemeanour (even though they are polite to him and always pay the rent on time)

We would all like pleasant neighbours that we get on with, but some such complaints raise issues in two respects:

1. How bad does behaviour have to be before it is considered anti-social?

2. Should landlords always be expected to listen to tell-tales or should the neighbours at times be prepared to have a word with the tenants who are, after all, their neighbours?

As a landlord, whilst you are not responsible per se for your tenants' behaviour, you do have a duty to see that tenants uphold the terms of the tenancy agreement, which should include terms such as the following, regarding anti-social behaviour:

1. Not to do or permit to be done in or about the Property any act or thing which may be or become a nuisance or annoyance to the Landlord or the occupiers of any neighbouring, adjoining or adjacent property …

2. Not to play music of any description… or to cause or permit any singing

or other noise to take place in the Property so as to cause annoyance to the Landlord or the occupiers or owners of any adjoining property or so as to be audible outside the Property between the hours of 11:00 pm and 7:30 am.

Neighbours do need to realise that landlords are not some kind of police force. It is illegal for landlords to harass their tenants. If a tenant disturbs the peace, the neighbours should first try to speak to the tenants and ask them to be more considerate. Neighbours will probably want to keep the landlord informed of any action they have taken or continue to take, but should also be prepared to accept responsibility for calling upon the police for assistance, or the environmental health department or other authority.

The role of the landlord is often one of mediation or balance between the tenants and neighbours. If the tenants are good as far as we're concerned, Dave will definitely not give them notice to quit purely on neighbours' say-so, if there is no supporting evidence. Caution should especially be applied to neighbours' complaints where there is any possibility of a racial element.

In most cases, Dave will make sympathetic noises to neighbours, offer to mention their comments to the tenants (if, as often, they wish to remain anonymous in their complaints) and, if appropriate, he will tell them to contact the police or other authorities.

Where there is firm supporting evidence of tenants being anti-social or repeatedly disturbing the peace, then Dave will inform the tenants firstly that he will give them notice to quit if the behaviour continues, and if it does, he gives them notice.

We have had incidents where neighbours phone to complain of a loud party and in this situation Dave phones the tenants to see what they have to say. Having admitted to the behaviour, he sends them a letter warning of the seriousness of this, along the lines demonstrated below:

Tenant Warning Letter

Dear XXXXX

Without Prejudice

Further to our telephone conversation today, I am writing to re-state the following:

Two of your nearby neighbours have contacted me today, to say that you had a party last night that was very noisy, went on until the early hours of the morning and kept many people awake. There was much litter in the street as a result of this party and damage to the grass verges (due to car parking) the next day.

I have spoken to the Environmental Health Department and the Housing Advice Department and they confirm I have a duty to ensure the reasonable behaviour of my tenants.

I would like to point out that this behaviour is in breach of your'tenancy agreement (clauses 3.14 and 3.15).

If this behaviour persists, I intend to serve you with Notice seeking possession of a property let on an assured tenancy, under Section 8 of the Housing Act, citing ground 14.

Yours truly,

David Bryant

Neighbours' comments can be constructive when they concern the property itself. For example, we appreciate them informing us if:

- Gutters or drains are blocked

- Joint flat roofs or down pipes cause problems

- The house is in any other way smashed up or damaged

- Any sign of vermin, squirrel trouble, etc

- Fences damaged or blown down

- Fire!

Tenants will often bring these things to our attention themselves, or Dave may find problems during his own inspection of a property. The police, fire brigade, council, or other authority may bring problems to our attention from time to time.

Neighbours may also speak to Dave when he is visiting a property.

Staying on the Right Side of the Law and not Harassing Tenants

It is of the utmost importance that as a landlord you understand - whether coping with any sort of problem behaviour by tenants or in the course of seeking to evict tenants (either on behavioural grounds or non-payment of rent) - that you must never in the eyes of the law harass your tenants. The only sensible course of action open to you at all times is staying on the right side of the law. It is important, therefore, to have some knowledge of what the relevant laws are.

Some landlords may find the stress of coping with tenant problems too much. If you find yourself in this position, it may be worth seeking support from any landlord organisation which you may (and should) belong to. They normally have a helpline. There are specialist agencies that will deal with matters for you, such as attempting recovery of rent and property from bad tenants, if you feel you need such support, although we consider that an unnecessary expense.

When the Rent is Late

Unless tenants have arranged to pay the rent by standing order, there may be times when they simply forget that rent day has come round again. A gentle word may at times be all that is required. When this happens with new or generally well-behaved tenants, Dave tries to approach the matter as diplomatically as possible in the first place, perhaps even bringing the subject up whilst phoning to discuss another matter. Good tenants will often be embarrassed about their forgetfulness. Dave might suggest it could be easier to set up a standing order mandate (this option will have been discussed when they took the tenancy, but we prefer to let them choose). It is a fallacy to assume that if tenants are paying by standing order your rent is assured, since it will still not be forthcoming if there are no funds in their account to support the payment and they can cancel the arrangement with their bank at any time.

Sometimes tenants' circumstances change and they may be experiencing genuine, temporary difficulties with paying the rent. For example, they may change jobs and now have a different payday, they are between jobs or one of a group of tenants may have moved out.

Tenants' Top Ten Excuses for Not Paying the Rent

1. I changed jobs and now get paid at the end of the month, that's why the cheque bounced.

2. I gave it to my friend to give to you, but he didn't pass it on.

3. I've been on holiday abroad.

4. I'm broke because it's my daughter's birthday.

5. I fell over and dislocated my shoulder and couldn't work last month.

6. I've moved out and now my unemployed sister is living there.

7. I had to give up my job because of depression. Now I have no money and it's really getting me down.

8. The other tenants moved out, which wasn't my fault, and I can't afford the rent (but believe I have the right to stay here).

9. The DSS should be paying you.

10. The tenant you normally talk to is in Gambia and the rest of us don't speak English

---

Non-Payment of Rent

It will soon become apparent if the rent is not forthcoming at all. You may phone the tenant on two or three occasions and get either no promise of rent or, more likely, only broken promises such as them arranging to meet you and not turning up, or saying "it's in the post" when it isn't. A cheque may turn up in the post, but bounce, being returned by the bank due to lack of funds. You will warn the tenant that if the rent is not forthcoming by the end of the week (by which time it may be going on for a month late), you will write giving them 14 days notice of your intention to commence court proceedings against them.

Dave would point out to the tenant involved at this stage that this would result in a CCJ (County Court Judgement) against them. Having a CCJ makes it hard for people to rent another property or get any form of credit. Many tenants will be keen to avoid this, and will either pay up or get out at this stage.

At no time should you as a landlord attempt to evict a tenant personally. It is an offence to manhandle a tenant, and can result in a prison sentence for you. Unless the tenant leaves voluntarily, the only course of action open is to take legal action. Some landlords may offer incentives for tenants to leave, but we don't do that.

After an undesirable tenant has moved out, it is always wise to change the locks at the property.

Steps to Evicting A Tenant

Tenants will sometimes leave voluntarily when they recognise that they cannot continue to pay the rent, or because other problems have arisen in relation to the tenancy. If, however, this is not the case and no reasonable solution can be found after discussing the matter with them, it will be necessary to:

Give the Tenant Legally Valid Notice

To legally end an Assured Shorthold Tenancy agreement, you must first serve a valid notice of your intention to seek possession, upon the tenant. Using one of the correct forms as outlined below, you will inform the tenant of the date by which you require them to leave the property, failing which you will apply to the Court for a possession order.

Importantly, in relation to Assured Shorthold Tenancy Agreements, the landlord can serve one of two different types of possession notice, commonly referred to as Section 8 and Section 21 Notices. The most widely used is the Section 21 Notice, as this does not require the landlord to specify any reason for ending the tenancy agreement.

> The good thing about a Section 21 is that it offers mandatory grounds for eviction, assuming it is correctly served. One small downside to Section 21 notices however, is that the court cannot grant a possession order to take effect sooner than six months from the commencement of the tenancy.

The good thing about a Section 21 is that it offers mandatory grounds for eviction, assuming it is correctly served. One small downside to Section 21 notices however, is that the court cannot grant a possession order to take effect sooner than six months from the commencement of the tenancy.

A Section 8 notice is served on specific grounds for breach of contract, including anti-social behaviour or non-payment of rent. Section 8 lists 18 possible grounds for eviction. Some of the grounds require two months notice, while others can be as little as two weeks. In the case of nuisance it can be immediate.

Section 8 Notice

I include Section 8 Notice requiring possession at Appendix VIII. Section 8 of the Housing Act 1988, specifies grounds upon which a landlord can claim possession of the premises. There are 18 separate grounds on which a landlord can seek possession. The first 8 grounds of the Section 8 Notice are mandatory, which means that if the landlord can show the Court that one of these grounds applies, the Court must give possession. The remaining grounds are discretionary, which means that the Court will not necessarily give possession, but will examine the situation as a whole and give a judgement which it considers to be just.

The most commonly cited grounds are for rent arrears, and you will see that rent arrears are covered in three grounds: 8, 10, and 11. Usually, it is best to choose all three; if the tenant is in sufficient arrears, choose ground 8 (being mandatory). You should read the grounds carefully before deciding which ones you wish to include in your Notice.

If, after serving a Section 8 Notice, the tenant still does not leave the premises, a Court order for possession will be required but it is imperative to serve the notice first.

Section 21 Notice

I include a Section 21 Notice requiring possession for a fixed term tenancy at Appendix IX and for a periodic tenancy at Appendix X. Section 21 Notices are by far the most common type of possession notice, and a landlord does not have to give any reason for ending the tenancy agreement, but simply serves the notice.

It is permissible to give a Section 21 for tenants to sign when they first take up the tenancy of a property (and it may be more difficult to get them to sign or acknowledge receipt of this later, when trouble arises).

There are two types of Section 21 Notice and the correct one must be served. These are the 'fixed term notice' and the 'periodic notice'. The difference between the two is quite straightforward. If the tenant is still in the fixed term of his tenancy, that is the tenancy agreement has not come to an end, then the fixed term notice needs to be served. Conversely, if the tenancy agreement has expired and the tenant is still in the property, the tenancy becomes a 'periodic tenancy' and therefore, the periodic notice needs to be served.

There are two categories of grounds for possession: mandatory and discretionary. It is advisable only to evict on mandatory grounds, as they are more straightforward. Under Section 21 of the Housing Act 1998, you can claim possession simply on the basis that:

- The tenancy was for a fixed period, which has expired and you want the property back.

- The existing tenancy is for an unspecified period (where the fixed term has expired and the tenancy has become 'periodic') and you want the property back.

- You have given your tenant at least two months written notice under the appropriate Section 21, informing him that you want possession of the rental property.

Under Section 8 in Schedule 2 of the Housing Act 1988, Mandatory Grounds for Eviction include:

- The tenant is in two months' rent arrears, both at the time of the service of the notice and the Court hearing.

When giving the tenant notice to quit (both for the Section 21 Notice and the Section 8), it is recommended that you hand the Notice to the tenant personally and get them to sign a copy of this. Alternatively, if sent by post, get a certificate of posting or send by registered post.

Take care over the date you give for requiring possession. A two-month notice period should expire on the last day of a 'period', where the first day of a period is the day on which rent is due. So the notice should be given in time (the day **before** the next rent day, for example) so it can expire at the end of two months on the day before the next rent is due (otherwise the tenant will have the right to stay until the end of the next period – up to the next rent day).

Make sure all paperwork is completed accurately, as judges will refuse a possession order on the grounds of any mistakes. If you belong to a professional landlords' association such as the NLA or NFRL, their helpline operators will be able to help you if you have any doubts.

Applying to the Court for Possession

If after the expiry of a valid notice to quit period the tenants remain in the premises, the landlord must still not attempt to evict them himself. Rather the landlord should make an application to the court for a possession order, which is a fairly straightforward form available from your local Court. It costs £120 to apply for a possession order.

You need to consider whether to submit a legal claim for the rent to be paid, or to simply go for accelerated possession of the property. It should be noted that claiming for unpaid rent will prolong the process and if the tenant simply cannot afford to pay you, the claim may well be unenforceable. It may be better to apply for accelerated possession to reclaim the property at the earliest date.

Accelerated Possession

An accelerated possession procedure enables tenants to be evicted without a Court hearing, purely on the basis of a written representation – which, of course, the tenant will be given the opportunity (for two weeks) to respond to. This procedure cannot include a claim for rent. It normally takes around 4 to 6 weeks for a possession order to be granted, and then the tenant will be given a couple more weeks by which time he must leave.

Non-Accelerated Possession Procedure

If you want to claim for unpaid rent, you cannot use the accelerated possession procedure and this alternative route normally takes longer. You may be required to appear in Court and the tenant will also be given the opportunity to dispute your claims.

If you do obtain a judgment against the tenant for payment but still do not receive payment, you can try to enforce the judgment by asking the Court for any of the following:

- A warrant of execution

- An attachment of earnings order

- A garnishee order

- A charging order

Details are obtainable from your local County Court.

When You Need to Get the Bailiffs In

If the Court grants you a possession order, they will send you a copy of the judgement as well as sending one to the tenant, stating the date by when the tenant must leave and possession of the property must be returned to you.

If the tenant still does not leave the property by the date the possession order dictates they should, you will have to apply via the Court for a bailiff to evict them. You will have to fill in another form and send another small fee to the Court for them to appoint a bailiff.

This will add another 3-6 weeks (times vary depending on the Court), before the bailiff turns up to evict the tenant.

On the day the bailiff goes in, you will need to be there to formally take possession and have a locksmith in attendance to change the locks unless you can do so yourself.

Excerpt from Dave's Diary...

Friday 12th March, 2004:

At 7.30 pm I booked someone in to 7M and took their money. They only gave me a month's deposit; they've promised me the other half a month on Sunday, so I'll have to go & collect it. I also went to 72C to fix a leak on their washing machine; I ended up just changing the washing machine and I spotted also that their drain was a bit slow running, so will go back on Saturday.

I served the section 8 Notice on 51B. A Section 8 Notice (ground 8) only takes two weeks before you can apply for a possession order unlike a Section 21, which takes two months.

In Summary

While it pays to be prepared for the downside, it should be remembered that it is not all doom and gloom having tenants! Look after your tenants and you will find that most are good and will refer other potential tenants to you. We find with over 60 properties, the chances are that at any given time we have at least one tenant giving us some degree of problem behaviour. We recently had an incident with what appeared at the time to be a tenant from hell, but that is passed now. Currently we have full occupancy of all our properties with one or two that are occasional late payers, but no non-payers.

Most tenants just want to get on with living peacefully in the property, although they will be straight on the phone to the landlord if the toilet leaks!

It's only too easy at times to wonder if you are getting it right with tenants. Things are bound not to be perfect all the time. If your tenants are too happy, you must be under-charging on the rent! It is a healthy sign if tenants recommend you to their friends and you have 'tenants waiting'.

In the final chapter of this book, I would like to round off by taking a look at overall planning and finding the inspiration to really go for it.

Chapter 9

Further Principles of Success

"The only limit to our realization of tomorrow will be our doubts of today. Let us move forward with strong and active faith."
Franklin Delano Roosevelt

Having read the preceding chapters, you now have enough information at your fingertips to successfully buy investment property, set it up and let it out. Property investing is such a solid long-term investment, it is difficult not to be a winner providing you know how to go about it, which you do after reading this book. So take action towards your own property investing success today!

Success requires careful planning and execution, the nuts and bolts of which have been examined throughout this book. It is important to remember that this applies equally whether you are setting out to buy your first investment property, or already have a sizeable portfolio. There's no point at which you are immune from making mistakes or errors of judgement.

When you do attain a level of success it is equally imperative as at the outset that you do not make major mistakes. It is possible to lose it all. Never forget that the more you have, the more you have to be careful about. I've met several investors who have built up sizeable portfolios then lost it all through sheer neglect, sometimes linked to what has been called too much testosterone... This syndrome (most common among men:-) often involves irrational deal fever (an over-attachment to the thrill of constant new deals, even when it is not wise to enter into them) and not enough focus on the nuts and bolts of running the portfolio that has already been accumulated!

Seriously, the optimum speed of growth for your portfolio will vary depending on market conditions, as well as personal and financial circumstances. Any decision about the number of properties you wish to buy in a given period will depend on the rate of growth this represents relative to your current position. Growth affects many factors, the most important being your cashflow.

It is advisable for any business to go through phases of greater and lesser growth, to ensure the business is sound. Add a new layer of growth and then pause to fortify the position. You must decide when the time is right for you to do this, as there is no set answer to the number of properties or the time when it will be right to pause for consolidation.

Your pace of growth will partly be affected by whether the type and location of the property is one with which you are already familiar. Often it is wise to stick to the KISS advice: Keep It Simple, Stupid! I have adopted the 'cookie cutter principle' whereby I buy properties of a type and in a location with which I am already very familiar.

When I began investing in property, I started slowly with one flat. After getting comfortable with that, I then bought four properties for each of the next three years. The following two years (with the children all now in school) I picked up the pace and started buying twelve properties a year.

When I bought 12 properties in 2002, (one of which is shown above) I previously had 13, so this more-or-less doubled my portfolio size. The financial stretch was large and had to be carefully managed; new properties inevitably represent a squeeze on profits, as they may involve increasing the mortgages on current properties as well as having initial set-up expenses and void periods. Our overall profit actually went down for the year when I doubled the portfolio, though this did not bother me, as Dave still had his day job at that point so I was not relying on the income and I understood this was just a temporary side-effect of rapid growth.

The following year, 2003, I bought 12 more properties but this time profits increased because the 12 new properties now represented only a 50 percent increase in the total portfolio size.

In 2004 and 2005 I slowed the pace to consolidate our position. I also felt it was time to find a new way to purchase properties and spent time learning how to buy below market value. It is important to be open to learning new strategies when market conditions change: I knew I had to do this because rents were not keeping pace with prices in our area. Dave had given up work by then as we had enough income from the properties to live, and I could afford to take my time learning new ways. Of course, you do not need to spend so long learning these new strategies as this book tells you all you need to know!

From 2006 onwards, I began to speed up the pace of buying again. We now own 61 properties and my goal is to buy a measured 10 properties a year for the next four years, to arrive at owning 100 properties. Some people won't be happy unless they're being inspired by someone who's bought 100 properties in one year but I believe my position is more solid and my equity and cash (my wealth) greater than most that have built such a stack of cards.

Before you go ahead with growing your portfolio, you should consider the current strengths and weaknesses of your property business. A useful technique for doing this is a SWOT analysis, that is an assessment of the:

Strengths

Weaknesses

Opportunities

Threats

The strengths and weaknesses refer to things that are internal to the business and opportunities and threats refer to external factors. You should undertake to make a regular 'position audit' or complete review, in each of these areas.

The internal **strengths** and **weaknesses** to consider include:

- Management skills

- The team of professionals and others who work with you

- Are you making best use of capacity (for example, have you considered setting up an HMO (house of multiple occupation) to increase income)?

- Are you doing enough research, marketing, or tracking the results of marketing?

- Profitability and financial performance, including the all important cash flow

External research should at least cover:

- Competition

- Political situation

- Economic situation

- Location

Opportunities may include:

- A change in government regulations

- A reduction in the interest rate

- A reduction in the number of competitors

- New areas found to invest in

- Contacts in new areas

- New financial arrangements available

Threats may include:

- Too many investors flooding the local market

- Large local employer leaving the area, or industry closing down

- Interest rates rising too high

- Falling house prices (depending on your current position)

- A new law restricting your business

- An economic recession

- The credit crunch!

Dealing with the risks and threats to your property business were discussed in Chapter 3, Planning and Risk Assessment.

With care, success through property investing can come more quickly than you anticipate. Your fortunes and lifestyle can change more quickly than your inner perceptions of reality and it is important to recognise there are key times when it is best to take stock.

If you want your property business to continue growing there may come a time when you need to make a decision to give up other paid employment and you must consider the lifestyle changes this will entail.

One of my favourite books on the subject of coping with business growth and change is The E-Myth Revisited by Michael Gerber. The gist of the message is that most entrepreneurs fail to grow their business because they are too busy going to work in the business, when they should go to work on the business.

Recognise that, as in any business, a huge shift in your beliefs is often required as your property business evolves, possibly from a simple job mentality (earn it = spend it), to a savings mentality (earn it = set some aside for tomorrow), to becoming an investor (earn it = learn to invest for a much brighter future), to a business mentality (stop thinking about 'earning it' = learn how to **make** money!)

You will also need to gain control over other fundamental concepts in order to complete your solid foundation for success. I believe that the most important areas we all need to work at mastering control over are self-discipline, goal setting and time management.

Self-discipline is a central concept that has a huge effect on how we live, as well as how successful we are. The diagram below shows the areas in which you must apply self-discipline in order to make the greatest progress in business and life in general.

Depending on your current position, age, and experience to date it is likely that you will find you excel in some of the areas above, do OK with others and perhaps need to do more work on the rest. I believe that you should aim to constantly work and improve on all of these areas.

Goal setting is another important concept. The two concepts of self-discipline and goal setting should act in harmony.

Having goals is very positive. For example, if you have a goal to buy your first investment property within the next six months, you are committing to a positive act. However, achieving this goal requires self-discipline and you will be less likely to achieve your goal if you do not work on any weak areas of self-discipline that may otherwise trip you up.

Self-discipline is not only about the things you must not do if you want to achieve your goals, it also encompasses identifying your strengths and weaknesses in all areas, so that you can leverage your strengths and work to build skills and abilities in the weaker areas.

It is important to hold the twin concepts of goals and self-discipline in balance - self-discipline without goals will not lead to happiness and success; neither will goals without self-discipline!

Time is said to be the currency of the 21st century and it is the one thing there never seems to be enough of. Alongside the twin concepts of goals and self-discipline, it is important to consider time management. How effectively you use your time will determine the progress you make in any field of endeavour.

You may have great goals and you may believe your self-discipline is under control, but it is surprisingly easy to develop bad habits relating to how you spend your time that you are barely aware of, and that may undermine your attempts to make progress. Possible culprits may include television watching, shopping and sleeping or chatting with friends more than is really necessary.

One of my favourite books on time management is Eat That Frog! by Brian Tracy. The twin concepts of self-discipline and goal setting are really drawn together in the book: time management is viewed as a form of self-discipline and eating a frog first thing in the morning is a metaphor for tackling your most challenging task first, the one you are most likely to procrastinate about. The book leads you through the steps to achieve greater effectiveness and success and to overcome procrastination, starting with the importance of written goals to gain clarity about what you want to achieve. Setting time deadlines is viewed as an important part of this process.

Related to time management and goals is **focus**: in order to succeed, you must have a long-term focus. Great achievements take time and you will never achieve great things unless you are prepared to set off on such long journeys. You will need to stay with problems and see things through. While writing this book, I had this quote tacked to my laptop which inspired me to stay on task:

"It's not that I'm smart, it is just that I stay with problems longer." Albert Einstein

One of the certainties of time is that it keeps rolling by. Our due diligence must always be weighed against the fruitlessness of procrastination. There will never be a perfect time to begin, to take action. It is worth remembering that the present, in many ways, is all we have: "The time is now!"

Another important aspect to success is motivation. You will not get very far in any endeavour without feeling **highly motivated** to accomplish the success. Think about your main motivation for wanting success. Write down what motivates you and keep it where you will be reminded daily.

It is not enough to faintly want success. You must have a strong desire to take the necessary actions, day by day, little by little, that success requires:

> *"It is the small decisions you and I make every day that create our destinies."*
> ***Anthony Robbins***

A key to finding sufficient motivation to succeed in your chosen field is to emotionalise your thoughts on the subject. We all operate under the pain/pleasure principle, which means that we seek to move away from pain and towards pleasure. By deliberately linking pleasure to your chosen subject, whether it be property investing or whatever, you will become motivated to want to work towards your goals in that area. Anthony Robbins discusses this in his excellent self-improvement books and CDs Unlimited Power and Awaken the Giant Within.

I believe that most people, before being capable of caring for a huge property portfolio responsibly, could do with gaining greater control of their personal spending and saving habits. If saving and investing are your weak points, I recommend Alvin Hall's books Your Money or Your Life and Money for Life which encourage you to keep a check on your spending and saving. There is also some excellent software available to help keep your finances in order, notably Microsoft Money.

Many businesses fail in their first year or two because of insufficient financial control. You need to have an understanding of the fundamental principles of book-keeping - how to set up accounts and how to benefit from the information contained therein. This may be a new skill you need to develop and it may be a good start to read a basic book on the subject such as Book Keeping Made Easy by Roy Hedges.

For many people, being better organised can be the key to a more successful and less stressful life. A very good general book on this subject is the Dorling Kindersley KISS Guide to Organising Your Life.

Many people go through life accumulating stuff that can end up being a nuisance and that clutters up their homes and lives unless they get it under control. Is this you?

I was guilty of hoarding tendencies myself until I read a very entertaining book on the subject Clutter's Last Stand by Don Aslett. It surprised me how taking the seemingly unrelated first step of de-cluttering helped me prepare for my new property venture.

Helen Foster's book Dejunk Your Life takes a broader look at the idea of de-junking as simplifying any area of life that doesn't fulfil or satisfy you, to make space for those things that will. This is considered for various areas of life: your surroundings, your image, your body, your time, your finances, your work, your stress levels, your mind, your love life and your social life. Very liberating!

For some of us the first step we may need to take before getting anywhere near success will involve overcoming personal struggles. This has been an important part of life's journey for me personally. I now appreciate that "God's delays are not God's denials" - it doesn't matter if you are late finding success in life, for you will be all the more grateful in finding success at all. I meet and mix with successful people on a daily basis, and success does not recognise age at all. Some meet success late in life and some are successful at twenty, or even younger!

One of the earliest books that really helped to turn my thinking around was Feel the Fear and Do It Anyway by Susan Jeffers. The book has been a huge worldwide success because it shows you, in simple terms, how to transform your anxieties into confidence, action and love.

We all need to have successful relationships with others to provide a solid foundation to any lasting success or happiness in our lives. It is difficult to focus on achieving success if you are racked with worry about a relationship that is broken or on the rocks, or indeed if you are experiencing too much stress as a parent. You could spend all your time worrying about relationships and get very little work done.

It is likely that many of your deepest values and desires do concern the key relationships in your life and these are always of compelling interest to all of us. An important book on this subject is Emotional Intelligence: Why It Can Matter More Than IQ by Daniel Goleman. Goleman suggests that emotional intelligence is the strongest indicator of human success. People who possess high emotional intelligence are the people who truly succeed in work as well as play, building flourishing careers and lasting, meaningful relationships. His second book Working With Emotional Intelligence, concentrates on relationships at work and is equally important.

In Conclusion

Ultimately, wealth is about being able to adopt a lifestyle that gives you the freedom to do what you want, when you want and to enjoy the good things in life that are really worthwhile.

Being rich will tend to magnify who you are and enable you to express yourself through how you choose to spend, save or invest your money and time. There is less opportunity for this freedom if you are financially challenged.

Money itself is neither good nor bad, but neutral. It is only when you get to the point where you can call yourself reasonably wealthy that you can truly appreciate what money is about. While each individual's experience will be different, most will agree that money has its own limitations in terms of what it can do for you. Your core values will not change when you have money. It is your values that keep you connected to what is most important; values such as love and charity. When you are rich, you will be able to have more time and freedom to give expression to your deepest values.

When you start out on the journey to make a fortune, you may believe that only when you arrive will your life be really good. Often it is only when you find yourself in a position where you feel you have arrived that you realise one of the most valuable things about getting to a position of being wealthy is, after all, the journey.

> *"Aim to become a millionaire for what it will make of you. What's important is the person you have to become in the process of becoming a millionaire."*
> **Jim Rohn**

What matters is that you are happy with yourself as well as with your life when you become successful and you consider how you undertook the journey, what you have done along the way and what you have become.

Don't ever stop trying to do and be the best you can. Stay inspired and eager, healthy and keen, for that is the essence of happiness!

Appendix I

Dave's Diary

I hope you will enjoy these excerpts from Dave's Diary, which serve to highlight the daily reality as a self-managing landlord with a large portfolio.

Excerpt from Dave's Diary...

Sunday 29th Feb:
Had a viewer at 10 o'clock at 7M and a viewer at 5 pm. Showed the 5 pm viewer 5R and 7M.

Monday 1st Mar:
Stripped the paper in the living room at 5R and painted it magnolia. Painted the ceiling of the kitchen and the ceiling of the hallway as well. That took most of the day.

Tuesday 2nd Mar:
Chased 24C for the rent. The viewer that I had at 10 am on Sunday came back to look at 7M. I had a 3 o'clock appointment with Bell's Boilers to fix the boiler at 7W and a 3.30 pm with Tom Bell for a gas safety check at 29P. I had to wait around until 6 o'clock, as I had a viewer then.

Wednesday 3rd Mar:
Working for the Salvation Army (9 am – 3 pm). Then I had three viewers at 4 pm – I showed them all 5R and 7M. Then I had to go and see Tim at 3H and give him a copy of the tenancy agreement, so he can claim housing benefit. Then at 6 o'clock I went to 57 B because they had a leak round their bath. At 7 pm I had another viewer at 7M.

Thursday 4th Mar:
Went to see Mary at 54E, gave her a refund that came from the council re her rent. At 11.30 am went to 15E to sign some paperwork so they can claim housing benefit. Had a viewer at 11 o'clock at 5R and 7M; had a viewer at 5 pm at 5R and 7M; took a deposit on 5R. Also went to 26S [this is one of my brothers' houses that we manage] and injected some leak sealer into their combi-boiler, because it keeps losing pressure. I also unblocked 57 B drain; I bought a set of drain rods and rodded it out, because there was water coming up through the back garden whenever she ran the tap.

Friday 5th Mar:
Salvation Army again. Made lots of phone calls late afternoon and had lots of paperwork. Including: we got summons re unpaid council tax at 3H that we did not know about! Also phoned Dennis at Southern Horizon about the damp at 3H.

Excerpt from Dave's Diary...

Saturday 6th Mar:

1 o'clock fixed the washing machine at 48D. At 2.30 pm 5 K left, so I went there to receive the keys and give them their deposit back. Chased 51 B for some rent. They've promised to pay me tomorrow, 7th March.

Monday 8th March:

I spent some time at 5 K putting a new time switch onto the immersion heater. Then I went to Crawley to collect some rent off a couple of people and also to dismantle a boiler that wasn't working properly. Then I had the carpets cleaned at 5K at 1 o'clock and at 6 o'clock I had my first viewer there.

Tuesday 9th March:

I had another viewer at 7 pm and one at 9 pm at 5 K. I also went to have a look at 26S boiler again, which was losing pressure, so I went to check that and I bled all the radiators. Then I went to 5R and 7M to collect Letsure forms that had been returned there. I spent the morning drilling out the heat exchanger from the boiler at 17B, which I had dismantled the day before.

Wednesday 10th March:

Went to work at Salvation Army, then I had two viewers at 7 o'clock and one at 7.30 pm at 5K. I also bunked off work for an hour and went to meet a builder at 3H to examine the damp problems there and they concluded that it's not the structure of the building; it's just the tenant's lifestyle. At 3 o'clock I went over to Crawley again, to 17B and put their boiler back together, with the new heat exchanger and I think they're happy.

Excerpt from Dave's Diary...

Thursday 11th March:

I spent the morning making phone calls, vetting applicants for 5R and 7M. I have promised 7M now to a woman who has quite a good employment history and quite a traceable accommodation history. She is going to meet me there tomorrow and sign the contract and hand over the money, so that will be good. She's got all her own appliances too, so she won't need anything at all – that's good news for me. Someone moved in to 5K at 3 o'clock- I took a deposit from them and got them to sign the AST. She's a very young girl only 20 years old, a post woman.

Friday 12th March:

At 7.30 pm I booked someone in to 7M and took their money. They only gave me a month's deposit; they've promised me the other half a month on Sunday, so I'll have to go and collect it. I also went to 72C to fix a leak on their washing machine; I ended up just changing the washing machine and I spotted also that their drain was a bit slow running, so go back on Saturday.

I served the Section 8 notice on 51B which I received in the post from the Southern Private Landlords' Association. A Section 8 notice only takes two weeks before you can apply for a possession order unlike a Section 21, which takes two months. You can only use the Section 8 when the tenant is at least two months behind with the rent, or has committed some other breach of contract.

Saturday 13th March:

At 11 am went to 57B to collect some rent and at 12 went to 72C to clear the drain, which I noticed the day before when I was changing the washing machine; I noticed it was a bit slow. When the washing machine pumps out, the water level rises in the sink. I also went to Taylor Robinson to collect the set of keys they had for us for 7M (which they were going to sell for us, but now we're keeping). I parked the car at 3H and had a quick look in there; Dennis Monroe hasn't cleaned it out (Housing Association handing it back to us). So I'm not very happy about that.

Excerpt from Dave's Diary...

 I also finally got council tax bills for 12R and 27A. The council are not going to charge me for the council tax between the time of buying it and letting it, because the places were empty and unfurnished (this differs from council to council; our council's rules are due to change new tax year).

I've already paid the 27A bill, because the council put it in the hands of a bailiff who threatened to charge me extra if I didn't pay. The council have now agreed to repay that and send me a refund.

Sunday 14th March:
Went to 33T to give them a new tenancy agreement and unblock their bath plughole. Also heard about how the man over the road has reported them to the police for "looking at him".

Monday 15th March:
Phoned the meter readings for 7M through to the gas and electricity boards, to get the account taken out of my name. At 6 o'clock I went back to 7M to collect the remainder of the deposit. At 6.30 pm I went to 3H with the people from 49G and they said they want it, even though it's all mouldy at the moment! Also during the day I went to 18T to fix the shower (it turned out she had just switched off the electricity supply to it!)

Tuesday 16th March:
At 3.30 pm I had a second viewing by someone at 5K; they had already given me a deposit, but they wanted the 'guarantor' to see the flat and to meet me. At 8 pm, I went to 130S to take them two single mattresses because their parents are coming to stay.

Wednesday 17th March:
At 3 pm I went to 17H, to fix their overflow again (for the third time). I ended up replacing the whole ball valve this time. I also met the people who are fitting the double-glazing there. At 3.30 pm met Tom Bell at 54E to do a gas test.

Excerpt from Dave's Diary...

Thursday 18th March:

I actually went to Brighton – I took the day off! Then at 7 pm, I went to 5K to move the girl in, drew up the tenancy agreement and took the money; gave her the keys and moved her in. Also got a phone call from Steve, who moved out of 3H, saying he would like to come back because he doesn't like it where he is; that's the second time he's moved out and wanted to come back!

Friday 19th March:

4 o'clock at 5R, moved the guys in (friends of Danny), took their money and gave them the keys. Then at 7 o'clock got a call from 130S saying could I take these mattresses and the sofa away, because they've bought a sofa bed. So I went and did that. Then at 9 pm, got a call from 5K – they had locked themselves out, so I had to go round there and let them in.

Saturday 20th March:

I delivered the sofa from 130S to 5K because they said they needed a sofa (they didn't have any furniture). At 2 o'clock I delivered a vacuum cleaner to 5R and fixed the loo at 7A; they had phoned me up an hour before and said the handle/flush is broken. Luckily I had a new one that I got out of a skip (!)

Sunday 21st March:

Had a call the night before from 7M saying their boiler wasn't working, so I went over there at 10 o'clock to fix it. They had just been mucking about with it and tried to turn it up and ended up turning it off! That was all.

Monday 22nd March:

I had an appointment to meet Dennis Monroe at 3H at 4 pm. The cleaner had been in earlier that day and made quite a good job of cleaning all the mould off the carpets and the walls. Dennis gave me the keys back and agreed to give me £350 to paint the place myself and after he had gone I actually started painting the ceilings.

Excerpt from Dave's Diary...

Tuesday 23rd March:
I was just painting 3H all day long. I went to 51B at 4 pm to collect the rent and when I got there he said he didn't have it for me, so that was a waste of time.

Wednesday 24th March:
I received a bill for the double glazing at 17H, but I'm not going to pay it yet because one of the windows is cracked, one of the vents is on the wrong way round and the mastic on the outside of the bathroom window is not in yet, because the overflow is leaking and the outside is wet and the mastic won't stick while it's wet. I phoned them up and said I'm not going to pay and they said "alright then"; they were quite happy with that.

Thursday 25th March:
I was working at 3H again, painting and at 12.30 pm we went to look at 11B - a house for sale. We offered on it, but the other interested party increased their offer to the full asking price.

Friday 26th March:
At 3 pm I went to 3H to finish off the painting. I ended up painting all of the walls and ceilings throughout the flat (2 bed flat) during the week and putting some new curtains up. At 4.45 pm, I met our tenants from 49G (who had seen it on Monday 15th and said they wanted it). I gave them the keys and a tenancy agreement. I dated it 20th so their rent day will remain the same and they started moving in. They will phone me sometime next week when they have finished vacating the flat at 49G.

Saturday 27th March:
At 53C one of the three has moved out and the two remaining are struggling to afford the rent. They only paid the full amount for the first few months, and then there have been shortfalls each month since the third person left. They have kept making excuses and saying someone new "might be moving in". I phoned them today and left a message. They haven't phoned back yet. Their tenancy ends anyway in April and I have told them I won't renew the tenancy agreement and will be giving them notice.

Excerpt from Dave's Diary…

 I spoke to Brian at 3H, because he owes me about 3 months' rent, which at £50 per week is only about £650 (We are sympathetic as he has been in hospital for depression, etc). He gave me some story about how he is waiting to put his claim in to the "Transport Benevolent Fund" (he lost his job "on the buses" due to his depression). I don't know why it is taking so long!

Sunday 28th March:
Went over to 26S at 9 am to fix their toilet that wouldn't flush and then I went to 53C because they haven't been returning my calls. There was no answer, so I waited outside in the car and I saw him coming in eventually so I went over and served him with the Section 21 notice and I actually got him to sign it as well. Then I phoned Brenda at 2R and agreed to meet her there at 1 o'clock and 'book her out'. I looked around the place, gave her the deposit back, she gave me the keys. I have decided to paint the small bedroom before handing over to Maria, on Tuesday.

Monday 29th March:
Painted the small bedroom at 2R.

Tuesday 30th March:
I went to 2R at 9 am and painted the kitchen ceiling and then at 12 o'clock someone moved in. I helped the tenants to move in. They just had a taxi to help them move from another house locally, but that wasn't enough, so I helped them with my car. The taxi and I did two trips each and I was there until about 2.30 pm.

Later, I had a phone call from 26S (one of my brothers' houses) saying they didn't have any hot water, so I went and fixed that. On the way back, I got a call from 17B saying they didn't have any hot water either, so I went and fixed that.

Wednesday 31st March:
Greenacres finally left. I delivered a vacuum cleaner to 2R actually; I promised them a vacuum cleaner. And I had a viewer at 49G at 5 pm that evening – friends of the people at 26S, including a girl called Sunshine. Later that night, about 8 pm, I went and bought a fridge for £20 for 49G.

Excerpt from Dave's Diary...

Thursday 1st April:
I worked at 49G. I put a washing machine in there and finished off the tiles in the kitchen, which a previous tenant had tiled but hadn't finished off properly.

Friday 2nd April:
At 5 o'clock I had Sunshine looking at 49G again and returning the forms to me. At 6 o'clock I had someone else looking at 49G. At 7 o'clock I went to 51B to meet Antonio who had promised to pay me some money and move out and Paula (a friend of his) who wanted to move in. She turned up but Antonio didn't. Then at 7.15 pm I got a call from him saying he'd left and that the back door was open and that the key was inside; so I went in, took the keys and locked up.

Saturday 3rd April:
I spent most of the day working at 51B, bagging up loads of rubbish and defrosting the freezer and sorting various things out. (Angela cleaned the kitchen, too!) At 12.30 pm I had a viewer at 49G.

Sunday 4th April:
The viewer for 49G yesterday phoned to say he had changed his mind, but I met Rebecca there at 10 am (previous viewer) and she gave me a deposit. Sunshine had already given me a deposit on 49G on Wednesday 31st, but she said she really wanted the house. So the plan now is to get her into 51B and Rebecca into 49G and not to have Paula (the friend of the previous tenant of 51B).

On Sunday 4th April I also went to 51B again, to do a bit of work there and found a BMX bike left behind in the shed (brought it home for the kids!)

Monday 5th April:
Bought a washing machine for £5 because it leaks and got a new pump for it for £27 and it works OK now.

Tuesday 6th April:
I went to 29P because their washing machine was leaking – the door seal was knackered. I also went to have a look at a washing machine in Crawley, but it was no good.

Excerpt from Dave's Diary...

Wednesday 7th April:
Rebecca moved in to 49G, so I had to go and check her in.

Thursday 8th April:
Chased Maurice for rent. Went to 57B for rent. Also fixed the washing machine that I got for £5, took it to Padstow and swapped it with their washing machine; took their old washing machine away and dumped it, after stripping the brushes and the pump off it – I always do that. Sunshine also moved in to 51B.

Friday 9th April:
Bank Holiday – didn't do anything!

Saturday 10th April:
Got a lawnmower for £20 and mowed the lawn at 2A. Also, I had to go to 3H to collect Maurice's rent.

Sunday 11th April:
Cut down some trees at 3H. They were growing very close to the house. I have found the easiest way to cut down trees (as I don't have a chainsaw) is not with a tree-saw, but using a drill – you can drill holes all round it until it falls over. So I cut them down, put them on the roof of the car and took them to the dump. There were three of them, about 12 ft tall. Also, gave our old computer table to 51B – to Sunshine.

Monday 12th April:
No property work!

Tuesday 13th April:
Went to the 15E AGM at Langley Green. Went to the dump again with more of the cut down trees. Also gave 51B a vacuum cleaner.

Wednesday 14th April:
I learned that 2K was being sold for £116,000 – we own 5K and 3K, which cost £33,500 in 1995 and £49,000 in 1999 respectively.

Thursday 15th April:
Chased 24C and spoke to 7A and 29C about imminent gas tests.

Excerpt from Dave's Diary...

Friday 16th April:
No appointments.

Saturday 17th April:
Collected the rent from 7 M.

Monday 19th April:
Chased 24C again and chased Southern Horizon about 3H – for the £350 for the re-decorating I did.

Tuesday 20th April:
Attended five gas tests with Tom Bell at houses in Bewbush. While I was at 5R I mowed the lawn for them and while I was at 2R I painted the living room for them. Also at 6 pm, I went to see a washing machine, which was for sale for £40 – I got it for a spare.

Wednesday 21st April:
No appointments.

Thursday 22nd April:
I cleared up the bin store at 15E – everyone was complaining about it at the AGM last Tuesday and saying how they have to pay extra to get it cleared up, but I just went round there and picked up a load of rubbish, including an old television set, and took it to the dump. I also started work on changing the water tank at 3H. I bought the new water tank and bought some pipe fittings and took them to 3H and left them in the empty bedroom.

Friday 23rd April:
I collected the rent from 51B.

Sunday 25th April:
Started working on installing the new water tank at 51B. I drained the system down, disconnected all the pipe work and removed the old water tank, put the new one in place and connected the pipe work. I then had to leave it overnight, for the sealant to dry. So overnight they didn't have any hot water, but they could use the shower and they didn't have any cold water, except at the downstairs loo and the kitchen. I also fixed a kitchen drawer at 51B that was coming apart.

Excerpt from Dave's Diary...

Monday 26th April:
Finished the water tank at 3H by refilling the tank and testing it; it seemed to be fine.

Tuesday 27th April:
Went to Brighton with Angela.

Wednesday 28th April:
6 pm – 4B's AGM at Henry Smith estate agents in the Carfax.

Thursday 29th April:
7.30 pm – Went to a Southern Private Landlords Association meeting at The Hawth in Crawley. Also went to Horley to collect the washing machine that I'd seen already, but they weren't ready for it to be taken.

Saturday 1st May:
Met the guy from 72C at Bewbush shops – he wanted me to give him notice so he could take it to the council and get higher up the waiting list! Also went to 6W to fix a leak on their water tank and to 57B because their lights weren't working. I found a loose connection in one of the light fittings – all the lights on one floor are wired in series so if one stops working, they all do. At 12 midday I went to 12T because their shower had stopped working. The solenoid had packed up – I don't know why they make showers with solenoids in!

Sunday 2nd May:
I replaced the electric shower at 12T – the new one cost £60.

Monday 3rd May:
I went to 6W again to sort out their leak and also to cut some trees down in their back garden. At 11am 8H left, so I went round there and read their meters, booked them out, gave them a deposit refund.

Tuesday 4th May:
Went back to 6W and finished the leak on the hot tank. At 4 pm, back to 57B again to fix the light in the loo this time – one of the prongs on the bayonet fitting had broken, so the light wouldn't stay in the socket and at 5 pm I had a viewer at 8H.

Excerpt from Dave's Diary...

Wednesday 5th May:
I had a viewer at 8H at 4pm and also put new floor tiles down on the kitchen floor over the old ones, which were horrible.

Thursday 6th May:
Had another viewer at 8H.

Friday 7th May:
No appointments.

Saturday 8th May:
Three viewers at 8H. Also chased Maurice for the rent. I also replaced the toilet cistern at 8H – the original cistern was a very old one made of cast iron (with a chain!) and it was rusting through and starting to weep. I replaced it with a low level plastic cistern. I used a siphon that has an integral overflow in order to avoid having to re-route the original overflow pipe work, because I didn't want to drill a 1 ½ " hole through the cavity brick wall just to put a new overflow in. I also went to 51B and 57B to collect rent.

Sunday 9th May:
Went to 3H to look at the under-floor heating, which isn't working. I'm probably going to get Martin Lee to install storage heaters there, so they can work on the cheap electric tariff.

Also had a viewer at 8H.

Monday 10th May:
Took Nearly's friend to see 8H. Also had two more viewers at 8 pm and 9 pm at 8H. My car failed the MOT.

Tuesday 11th May:
Worked on my car.

Wednesday 12th May:
Salvation Army and also collected a deposit for 8H from Nearly's friend at 6W. Her name is Unis.

Thursday 13th May:
Went to Brighton with Angela and also got a phone call from 48D asking me to cut their hedge, so I went and did that.

Excerpt from Dave's Diary...

Friday 14th May:
Salvation Army. Took the car to the garage to have some work done.

Saturday 15th May:
Had welding done on the car. Got a bed for 8H, second hand and delivered it. Also went to 3H and fixed their door that wouldn't shut properly which involved taking it off and planing wood off it.

Monday 17th May:
Had a new windscreen fitted and passed my MOT re-test.

Tuesday 18th May:
Painted the bathroom at 8H, even though I had already taken a deposit on it – it was hideous. And mowed the lawn. Also bought, second hand, a freezer to go into 7W. They are going to be leaving in a few days' time and it's going to need a freezer.

Wednesday 19th May:
Got a call from 23SH, saying, "the lights don't work", so I went round there and replaced the fuse. Also got a call from 5K, saying, "the hot tap won't turn off", so I went round there and replaced the tap washer.

Thursday 20th May:
Put a second coat of paint on the 8H bathroom and also got a call from 48D saying their lawnmower wouldn't work. I went and looked at it and it's knackered, so I just got them a new mower – you can get one for £20 from Argos.

Friday 21st May:
Salvation Army. That's it.

Saturday 22nd May:
Got a phone call from 4T saying their freezer is broken and he needs a new one. Went to have a look and it was just blocked up because he has never defrosted it. I defrosted it and now it's fine. He was saying: "but it needs to have that ice in there, otherwise how will it cool the food?" He did not understand how it works.

Excerpt from Dave's Diary...

Sunday 23rd May:
No call-outs!

Monday 24th May:
Gas tests at 8H and 36H. While we were at 8H I mowed the lawn and at 36H I noticed that the sink was hanging off the wall – they hadn't bothered to tell me about it, so I need to do that. The gas inspector noticed that the thermostat on the boiler at 36H wasn't working. It was getting ever so hot before the over-temperature thermostat was cutting out. You have to press the reset button to make it come back on again. So we need a new thermostat there.

Tuesday 25th May:
The inspector noticed the combi-boiler was losing pressure so it must be leaking from somewhere. I replaced the toilet seat while I was there as well, because they'd complained to me that the old one was split.

10 am: Someone moved in to 36H.

Wednesday 26th May:
Salvation Army.

Thursday 27th May:
Christopher went to New York, so I had to take him to meet his Nan at Heathrow Airport.

I bought a second-hand fridge-freezer.

Friday 28th May:
Took my car to the garage to have the wheel bearing done.

Salvation Army.

Also, went over to 57B to fix the leak around her bath yet again!

Saturday 29th May:
John Allen left 7W at 5 pm so I went there for the property hand-over and to give him his deposit money back and collect the keys.

Excerpt from Dave's Diary...

I also went to 15E – they've got cockroaches! I put down some insect powder, which seemed to be working and told them to get in touch with the council if their problems continued with the cockroaches. The seal around their fridge is a bit knackered as well, so I gave them the one I bought the other day and took their old one to the dump.

I also went to 53C at 6 pm to collect the rent.

Sunday 30th May:
Went to Haywards Heath and got a fridge/freezer for £40 for 7W. The tenants that just moved out had their own, so I needed to get one for the new tenants.

Also, I had three viewers at 7W, at different times throughout the day.

Monday 31st May:
I got a fridge-freezer locally for only £10 – I don't need it for now, but I'll store it in the workshop.

Tuesday 1st June:
I met the tenant from 4B in the shops just by chance. He said that his television does not work and that he can only watch videos. He has been living there for a few months, but had not bothered to phone me about it. I went round there and it turned out he hadn't plugged the aerial into the socket on the wall right behind the television.

Wednesday 2nd June:
Salvation Army. Later, I met the council surveyor at 7W so that he can satisfy himself that the place is unfurnished, so that I get a council tax exemption.

Thursday 3rd June:
No call-outs!

Friday 4th June:
Salvation Army and I got beds for 7W from the Salvation Army!

Saturday 5th June:
Matthew's party with a bouncy castle!

Excerpt from Dave's Diary...

Sunday 6th June:
Chris returned from New York and Jack & Betty visited. I picked them up from the airport.

Monday 7th June:
I met Barry at 7W at 2 pm to clean the carpets, £65. I said he could help himself to tools and things that had been left in the shed there.

Tuesday 8th June:
I collected the rent from 57B. I also fixed the mastic around her bath yet again, because she'd had a shower before it was dry and washed all the mastic away. She denied it, but I could see that must have happened.

Wednesday 9th June:
Salvation Army.

I put new brake pads on my car.

Thursday 10th June:
I went to 7M at 10 am to collect the rent. At 4 pm I had a gas test at 15E. Also mowed the lawn at 7W.

I also put new master brake cylinder seals on my car.

Friday 11th June:
Salvation Army.

Saturday 12th June:
At 1 pm I went to 3H because they had a leaking pipe under the sink and also a dripping tap, so I fixed that. At 2 pm I went to 7M to collect more rent because they hadn't paid me enough before. When I got there, they got me to connect their cooker – they have been there three months and they haven't had a cooker. It's their own electric cooker, but they don't know how to connect it.

Appendix II

Property Viewing Checklist

Property Viewing Checklist

OUTSIDE THE PROPERTY:

- Is it on a busy road?

- Is it on a flight path?

- Is there parking outside or nearby? (and is this allocated?)

- Are there any roof tiles missing?

- Are there cracks in the walls or other possible signs of subsidence?

- Are there any nearby trees?

- Any damp or mould patches around drains and gutters; signs of water leakage?

- Signs of rot in the window frames?

- What's the condition of the path, drive and garden?

- What are the immediate neighbours' houses like? (try to meet the neighbours if you want to)

INSIDE THE PROPERTY:

- Are there any internal signs of subsidence (such as large cracks in plasterwork)?

- Are there any signs of damp?

- Does the property require any major refurbishment work or alterations to make it suitable to let?

- Have the current owners very recently decorated? (new paint or paper could conceal damp or other problems!)

- What is the general standard of decorative order and will the property require re-decorating?

- Does the property require any other substantial improvements such as a new kitchen or bathroom? (The absence of a shower should not be too much of a problem, as one can be installed. Some tenants do not mind having no shower and they can cause problems - worth considering!)

- Is the loo separate from the bathroom? This is an advantage for sharers and a downstairs loo, while not essential, is a welcome bonus!

- Are the windows in good condition? Or double-glazed? (We do not insist on double-glazing for our properties; without which the property should be cheaper to buy. The windows may be adequate for comfort as they are and besides can be replaced later if required.

- What type of flooring is there and is it in good condition?

- What heating system is there and is it adequate to centrally heat the whole property? Look at the condition of the boiler and ask to see any service history.   We do not insist on having radiators, which some people do. We have warm air heating in our own home and are quite happy with it, and many of our investment properties are happily let with this too. It can be cheaper to buy such a property.

- Think about the size of the smallest bedroom. Especially with a three-bedroom house, these can be so small as to be of little use to anyone but a baby!

- If you are getting a two bedroom flat for sharers, also consider the size of the second bedroom; it is better to get two more equally sized bedrooms. Some two-bed flats 'assume' a family, with a large lounge and small second bedroom - not favourable proportions for sharers.

- A big two bedroom flat may be suitable for conversion to three bedrooms, depending on the layout. Each bedroom will be required by law to have a window and this will limit the layouts that are possible.

- Is the kitchen big enough for a dining table, or if it is a full kitchen/diner, could this space usefully be divided to give an extra room?

- Is there a self-contained lounge that could double as extra bedroom?

- Electrics - if the sockets are old type, the whole place is likely to need rewiring.

- Gardens - most tenants prefer a small, low maintenance garden (as do most landlords!)

- Parking - whilst this is always desirable I have heard that in some areas of London, particularly, a premium of up to £80,000 on the price of properties can be paid for the privilege of off-street parking and this is hardly likely to be reflected in the rent achievable. We have houses with no parking directly outside and they let for the same rent as those with closer parking places, and can be cheaper to buy. Of course, some people will not go for the property, but it is a question of knowing the demand

Appendix III

Budget Analysis for Buy to Sell Project

Budget Analysis for Buy to Sell Project

Purchase Price		£150,000.00
Sale Price		£178,000.00
GROSS PROFIT		**£28,000.00**
LESS EXPENSES		
Nature of Expense	**Investment**	**Cost**
PRE-COMPLETION COSTS		
Land Register - Property Title		£2.00
Realtime valuation on the house		£40.00
Lender's property valuation		£75.00
Lender's administration fee		£431.80
Lender's telegraphic transfer fee		£25.00
Solicitor's legal costs		£200.00
DMH (Solicitor) search fee		£109.36
Obtain and supply results of environmental search		£29.00
DMH CHAPS transfer fee		£40.00
Administration fee		£55.00
VAT on the above: solicitor's legal costs etc		£75.84
Stamp Duty Land Tax		£1,500.00
Land Registry fees payable for registration		£150.00
Land Registry search fee by solicitor		£4.00
Land Charges search fee by solicitor		£4.00
Telegraphic transfer of deposit etc to solicitor		£25.00
Buildings insurance for six months (approx)		£100.00
Pay seller's legal fees		£500.00

SUB-TOTAL COSTS PRE-COMPLETION		**£3,366.00**
(not inc. lender costs added to loan)		
Plus investment of DEPOSIT FOR PROPERTY	£22,500.00	
TOTAL MONEY TO BE PAID PRE-COMPLETION		**£25,866.00**
POST COMPLETION COSTS		
AQS fees at max £1,500 + VAT 17.5%		£1,762.50
Mthly mtgge on £129,956.80 x 6 mths @ £739.70		
Freedom Tracker (no rpp) at 6.937% interest		£4,438.20
Council Tax (assume 50% reduction) - 6 mths, est		£200.00
Re-carpet and fitting for lounge/stairs/landing		£300.00
Re-decoration costs		£100.00
Miscellaneous maintenance costs (fixing stuff!)		£100.00
Utilities (gas, electricity, water)		£200.00
Sub-total of costs during time of ownership		£7,100.70
TOTAL MONEY WE NEED TO HAVE AVAILABLE		**£32,966.70**
COSTS UPON SALE OF PROPERTY		
Estate agent's fees @ 1.5%		£2,670.00
Solicitor's costs (all inclusive) upon sale, approx		£500.00
Accountant's costs		£250.00
Sub-total of selling costs		£3,420.00
Total costs		**£13,886.70**
NET PROFIT (Gross profit less total costs)		**£14,113.30**

Appendix IV

Bryant Property Lettings Ltd

Business Plan
(January 2003)

This plan was requested by one of our lenders, when we reached a point of asking to borrow over one million pounds from them and we were also asking to borrow in the name of our new limited company, which we had just incorporated.

As submitted to our mortgage lender

Business Plan

1. Who We Are:

Name of business: Bryant Property Lettings Ltd

Business address:

Postcode:

Telephone no:

Telephone no:

Date business commenced: 10/01/2003 (incorporation date)

Legal status: Limited Company

Principal activities:

To buy to let three properties initially with 85 percent mortgages from [the lender]. Deposits will be drawn from equity in currently owned properties. The three properties to be purchased will be let at rents of £650 - £700 per calendar month and we will manage them ourselves, as we do our present properties.

2. Business Objectives:

The short-term objectives of the business:

We are aiming to achieve positive tax planning advantages by setting up this limited company, with the guidance of our accountant. We will be concentrating on the smooth administration and running of this new company. We will also consider integrating the running of some or all of the properties we already own within the framework of our new company.

We aim for the company to be as financially buoyant as our current buy to let properties have so far proved to be.

The medium term objectives of the business:

Depending on market conditions as time goes by, we will either hold or expand the number of properties we own.

When we feel it is required, Mr Bryant aims at some point to make the maintenance and management of the properties his full time occupation, since we have already reached the point where our properties provide a sustainable income for each of us which is greater than the original 'day job' incomes.

When Mr Bryant is in a position to manage the properties full-time, this will enable our further expansion to develop more fully.

The long-term objectives of the business:

We may possibly consider expanding into other areas of property investment such as commercial property, or look to investing in areas further afield, depending on market conditions.

Finally, we hope to be able to keep some of our properties for our lifetime at the end of the mortgage terms, by selling some at sufficient profit to finance paying off the mortgages on the remainder. These will then effectively provide us with a retirement income and something for the children to inherit!

Key risk areas:

a)   Weaker demand for rental properties

b)   Falling property values

c)   Rises in interest rates

Contingency plans for key risk areas:

a)   We have sufficient margins to lower rents

b)   We will wait for long-term recovery

c)   We will raise rents if required and if possible

3. Key Personnel:

Details of key personnel in the business:

Name (1):   Mr David Bryant

Position: Director

Academic/professional qualifications:

HND Mechanical Engineering and BSc Engineering

Experience and knowledge of your industry:

David Bryant has managed and maintained our 25 plus properties so far owned, very well. He is a natural handyman and gifted with an unusual amount of commonsense and integrity. He is confident in his dealings with tenants, as well as being understanding and fair. He can also remain detached and calm when required, for example if a tenant is not paying the rent. He is also excellent with budgeting and with keeping expenses to a minimum.

Name (2):   Mrs Angela Bryant

Position: Director and Company Secretary

Academic/professional qualifications:

BSc (Hons) Psychology

Post-graduate Certificate in Business Studies

Experience and knowledge of your industry:

I, Angela Bryant, have been the driving force behind the planning for the purchase of our properties. I have previously worked in administrative jobs, which have helped develop my organisational skills. I have spent several years studying relevant and related areas of investment and business and personal development, which have provided great support and guidance for all our plans.

Contingency plans, if key personnel are unable to work through illness or injury:

If one of the directors were unable to work, we would aim to employ extra help as necessary. We have support networks for further help at the properties or at home, which we normally use on a minimum basis to save on costs, but which we know we can turn to. This would be for handyman services; home help/childcare; administrative or other support as required. We believe we have the financial capacity as well as the contacts to deal with any eventuality. We could consider turning over the management of the properties to a letting agent in extreme circumstances!

4. Premises:

Describe the business premises and whether the premises will be sufficient for future needs:

We intend to remain home-based. We believe our home provides a perfectly adequate base for our business. Our home is a good-sized four-bedroom detached house with plenty of office space available for the paperwork and administrative needs of our property business.

We recently added a large workshop, which is helpful for the storage of decorating and maintenance equipment and some carpet and kitchen appliance storage for the properties.

5. Pricing:

Describe the basis for calculating prices – in this case the rents:

We keep a careful watch on the rents being asked for by letting agents and other private landlords (via local papers, internet and personal research). We also place advertisements as our properties become available and monitor the response to these. We are always willing to be flexible within reasonable limits in accordance with response levels, aiming to fill properties as quickly as possible.

6. Customers:

Who, where and how many potential customers does the business have?

We always find we have several calls in response to our advertising (ranging from half a dozen to over a dozen); not all of these will wish to take matters as far as actually renting the property concerned. We analyse the responses and this can also give guidance as to future property purchases.

We are open-minded about potential tenants with regard to their grouping, careers, race, language, history and so on. We feel this is much appreciated by many good people who shy away from letting agencies.

What are the strengths of the business that will influence customer decisions to prefer to come to us?

We do not make any administrative or other extra charges to tenants. We are also open all hours and days, for receiving enquiries and viewers, as well as for attending to maintenance and management issues and emergencies.

Outline any market research that has been undertaken to demonstrate a demand for the service:

We have been letting properties locally for a few years now and continue to monitor the levels of demand and supply regularly. We believe that the airport in particular, on which the local economy is largely based, employs a high level of contract workers; this in turn supports a healthy rental market, with many in temporary employment wishing to rent rather than buy property. Both local towns in which we invest have strong economies, with traditionally low levels of unemployment, high average earnings and strong demand for housing.

7. Competition:

Who are the major competitors and where are they based?

We are aware that others like ourselves have entered into buying property to let and this has led to increasing numbers of properties available to rent. At the same time, this supply has partly been absorbed by a growing demand. On balance, rents have not increased by much in spite of a doubling of house prices over the last five years. This has led to tighter profit margins, but still leaves room for a positive cash flow and we believe the capital appreciation justifies the reduced profit.

What are your strengths and weaknesses and those of competitors?

We feel that our experience and solid asset base makes us stronger than many of our competitors who are buying to let. Also, our commonsense approach to keeping expenses minimal, including the self-management of our properties. We believe that many buy to let landlords feel uncomfortable outside of their own standards in choice of neighbourhood, tenants and décor, thus many of them are fishing in the same expensive and small pond – whereas we take a niche position at the bottom end of the market, where there is always a strong demand and less competition.

Unlike many other landlords, we are prepared to accept DSS tenants and also plan on leasing properties to a housing association for a five year period with rent guaranteed and no voids.

Is the market static, declining, growing, or seasonal and why?

Demand for rental property has increased due to rising property prices and general demographic trends.

In terms of property prices, the long-term history of the property market tells us that it is a cyclical market and we are of course aware that given the strong growth over the last few years there is potential for future falls. However, our view is that there is room for further growth presently, given low interest rates and unemployment. We anticipate riding out any future storms that may come by simply holding with the properties through any storm and hoping this might clear the air of some weaker competitors.

8. Financial information – start-up businesses:

What are the total start-up costs?   £349,000

What is our personal contribution?   £52,350

9. Cash flow Forecast for the Business's First Year

See attached Spreadsheet for the cash flow forecast figures, which indicate a net annual profit for the three properties of £6,656 for the first year. Of course, we would expect this to increase in subsequent years after recovering from start-up costs.

Appendix V

Bryant Property Lettings Ltd

Cashflow Forecast

(January 2003)

Cashflow Forecast (January 2003)

From April 2003 - April 2004

Description	APRIL '03	MAY '03	JUNE '03	JULY '03	AUG '03
Property One:					
RENTAL INCOME		£650.00	£650.00	£650.00	£650.00
Expenditure:					
Set-up/decorating costs	-£70.00				
Communal maintenance/ insurance/					
Ground rent	-£75.00	-£75.00	-£75.00	-£75.00	-£75.00
Repairs/maintenance	-£50.00			-£50.00	
Admin and Advertising	-£20.00	-£2.00		-£2.00	-£2.00
Finance costs: Mortgage	-£386.40	-£386.40	-£386.40	-£386.40	-£386.40
Property Two:					
RENTAL INCOME		£700.00		£700.00	£700.00
Expenditure:					
Set-up/decorating costs	-£50.00				
Buildings insurance	-£13.50	-£13.50	-£13.50	-£13.50	-£13.50
Repairs/maintenance/gas test	-£50.00			-£50.00	
Admin and Advertising	-£20.00	-£2.00	-£2.00	-£2.00	-£2.00
Finance costs: Mortgage	-£438.21	-£438.21	-£438.21	-£438.21	-£438.21
Property Three:					
RENTAL INCOME		£650.00	£650.00	£650.00	£650.00
Expenditure					
Set-up/decorating costs					
Communal maintenance/ insurance/					
Ground rent	-£67.92	-£67.92	-£67.92	-£67.92	-£67.92
Repairs/maintenance/gas test	-£50.00			-£50.00	
-£2.00	-£2.00	-£2.00	-£2.00	-£2.00	-£2.00
Finance Costs: Mortgage	-£387.94	-£387.94	-£387.94	-£387.94	-£387.94
OPENING BANK BALANCE:	**£2,000.00**	**£231.03**	**£856.06**	**£1,481.09**	**£1,956.12**
Closing Bank Balance:	**£231.03**	**£856.06**	**£1,481.09**	**£1,956.12**	**£2,581.15**
First Year, Net Annual Profit: £4,656.36	**£6,656.36**				

Notes: We make the assumption that all the properties' purchases complete April 2003 and that they each take one month to become occupied. We will provide an opening bank balance of £2,000 (which we could increase) to allow for the initial void period and setting up costs.

SEPT '03	OCT '03	NOV '03	DEC '03	JAN '03	FEB '03	MAR '03
£650.00	£650.00	£650.00	£650.00	£650.00	£650.00	£650.00
-£75.00	-£75.00	-£75.00	-£75.00	-£75.00	-£75.00	-£75.00
	-£50.00			-£50.00		
-£2.00	-£2.00	-£2.00	-£2.00	-£2.00	-£2.00	-£2.00
-£386.40	-£386.40	-£386.40	-£386.40	-£386.40	-£386.40	-£386.40
£700.00	£700.00	£700.00	£700.00	£700.00	£700.00	£700.00
-£13.50	-£13.50	-£13.50	-£13.50	-£13.50	-£13.50	-£13.50
	-£50.00			-£50.00		
-£2.00	-£2.00	-£2.00	-£2.00	-£2.00	-£2.00	-£2.00
-£438.21	-£438.21	-£438.21	-£438.21	-£438.21	-£438.21	-£438.21
£650.00	£650.00	£650.00	£650.00	£650.00	£650.00	£650.00
-£67.92	-£67.92	-£67.92	-£67.92	-£67.92	-£67.92	-£67.92
	-£50.00			-£50.00		
-£2.00	-£2.00	-£2.00	-£2.00	-£2.00	-£2.00	-£2.00
-£387.94	-£387.94	-£387.94	-£387.94	-£387.94	-£387.94	-£387.94
£2581.15	**£3,206.18**	**£3,681.21**	**£4,306.24**	**£4,931.27**	**£5,406.30**	**£6,031.33**
£3,206.18	**£3,681.21**	**£4,306.24**	**£4,931.27**	**£5,406.30**	**£6,031.33**	**£6,656.36**

Appendix VI

The Buying Process: England & Wales

The Buying Process: England & Wales

1. Decide where you wish to buy and what type of property you are after.

2. Choose a mortgage and get an offer in principle.

3. Begin your search for a property in the area you want, through registering with estate agents and any other means you wish to try.

4. Find a solicitor/conveyancer who is willing to act for you and who is acceptable to your lender.

5. When you find a property you want to buy, make an offer (through the estate agents if used).

6. Often you may begin with a low offer, the vendor will request more and you will meet somewhere in between.

7. Once your offer is accepted, this is normally confirmed in writing by the estate agent (where applicable) who will also send a copy to your solicitor, giving details of the vendor's solicitor.

8. Your solicitor will then contact the seller's solicitor, to request title deeds to the property and to begin contract negotiations.

9. You will also submit your mortgage application form (through your broker, where used).

10. The mortgage lender will ask to carry out a valuation and survey, or homebuyer's report, to be carried out on the property.

11. When the mortgage lender receives the valuation report they will consider this along with your mortgage application and make you a mortgage offer (or not) dependent on the results of these.

12. If work is deemed necessary at the property, the lender may make a retention on the mortgage – holding back an amount equivalent to the estimated cost of works. This may involve some negotiation with yourself.

13. The solicitor will then consider the mortgage offer and survey results.

14. The solicitor will also carry out local authority and environmental searches, which you normally pay for upfront.

15. Solicitor also investigates the property title and other issues, including asking the purchasers how they wish to own the property, either as tenants in common (in equal or unequal shares) or as joint tenants (which you may wish to discuss with a probate solicitor). Or you may be buying as a limited company (which involves extra work!)

16. If all is in order, the solicitor will draw up contracts and send you all the legal paperwork.

17. If you are satisfied with the paperwork and assuming you have by now received confirmation of your mortgage offer, you sign the contract together with others you may be buying with and state any preferences of dates for completion.

18. The solicitors exchange contracts on behalf of you and the seller. At this stage, you are legally committed to the purchase and you will normally be required to pay 5% or 10% of the purchase price as deposit (the remainder of the deposit to be paid by completion).

19. A date for completion is agreed and the solicitor will make sure the mortgage funds will be available for the completion date, then exchanges contracts with the seller's solicitor and sends them your deposit.

20. The solicitor prepares the transfer of title deeds, which is signed by you and lodged with the seller's solicitor until the completion date.

21. The mortgage lender transfers money to your solicitor's account in time for completion.

22. You will also be required to pay the remaining deposit and often the solicitor's bill in time for funds to clear before completion.

23. The solicitor transfers the money to the seller's solicitor on the completion date, in return for the transfer deed, Land Registry certificate and keys. The sale is completed on your completion date.

24. The solicitor arranges for the transfer deed to be stamped, pays the stamp duty and sends the transfer deed to the Land Registry, to record you as the owner.

25. The solicitor arranges for the title deed to pass to your mortgage lender as security for the loan.

Appendix VII

How the Property Buying Process Differs in Scotland from England & Wales

How the Property Buying Process Differs in Scotland from England & Wales

England and Wales:

Step 1:

You see a property, usually advertised through estate agents or others.

Step 2:

Make an offer subject to the terms of the sale contract, taking a lead from the guide price in the property particulars - normally at or below the advertised price – in discussion with the estate agents.

Step 3:

If the sellers are agreeable to the offer, you will receive notice that they are willing to accept the offer subject to the terms of the sale contract.

Step 4:

Apply for a mortgage. You pay for the building society or bank's mortgage survey and valuation report, which you are entitled to see. If necessary, arrange for a Housebuyers Report or Survey.

Step 5:

Solicitors will be instructed and your solicitor will prepare a draft contract and a list of preliminary enquiries to send to the seller's solicitor.

Step 6:

The solicitors exchange letters and enquiries. Your solicitor will arrange for and receive local searches.

Step 7:

When everybody is happy with the contract, your solicitor will prepare a report on title and arrange to see you to discuss their findings.

Step 8:

Following these enquiries, each party's solicitor will arrange for their clients to sign copies of identical contracts.

Scotland:

Step 1:

You see a property that is advertised for sale – often by solicitors. They combine the roles occupied by estate agents and solicitors in England.

Step 2:

Decide the price you are prepared to pay, taking a lead from the upset price and from your solicitor who will know the local area.

Step 3:

Ask your solicitor to note an interest in the property. This indicates that you are interested and wish to be kept informed of developments.

Step 4:

Apply for a mortgage and pay for the lender's survey and valuation report. If necessary, arrange for a Housebuyers Report or Survey.

Step 5:

Your lawyer prepares an offer to send to the seller's solicitor, including title, movables, the searches on land, and a deadline for acceptance.

Step 6:

The seller decides whether the price is acceptable and their solicitor addresses each clause in the offer. Then they write back to your solicitor with a qualified acceptance and their own conditions of sale. There may be a series of letters negotiating the sale - this process is known as negotiation of **missives.**

Step 7:

Decide if the conditions of the sale are acceptable and ask your solicitor to issue an acceptance. This is known as **conclusion of missives** and a binding contract exists.

Step 8:

The seller sends the title deeds to your solicitor who draws up a new title deed known as a **disposition**. Your solicitor then conducts a property search to check the title is marketable, and obtains the property enquiry certificates – the equivalent of searches south of the border.

Appendix VIII

Section 8 Notice Requiring Possession of a Property

SECTION 8 NOTICE

Housing Act 1988

Section 8 as amended by section 151 of the Housing Act 1996

NOTICE SEEKING POSSESSION OF A PROPERTY LET ON AN ASSURED TENANCY OR AN ASSURED AGRICULTURAL OCCUPANCY.

Please write clearly in **black** ink.

Please tick boxes where appropriate and cross out text marked with an asterisk (*) that does not apply.

This form should be used where possession of accommodation let under an assured tenancy, an assured agricultural occupancy or an assured shorthold tenancy is sought on one of the grounds in Schedule 2 to the Housing Act 1988.

Do not use this form if possession is sought on the "shorthold" ground under Section 21 of the Housing Act 1988 from an assured shorthold tenant where the fixed term has come to an end or, for assured shorthold tenancies with no fixed term which started on or after 28th February 1997, after six months has elapsed. There is no prescribed form for these cases, but you must give notice in writing.

1. To:

Name of Tenant: ....

2. Your landlord/licensor* intends to apply to the Court for an Order requiring you to give up possession of:

Address of the Premises...

....

Postcode: ....

3. Your landlord/licensor* intends to seek possession on the following ground(s) in Schedule 2 to the Housing Act 1988 as amended by the Housing Act 1996 which read(s):

....

....

....

....

Continue on a separate sheet if necessary:

Use the Statutory text when completing paragraph 3 for the ground or grounds upon which you, as the landlord, are seeking possession of the premises. A full list of the grounds contained within the Act is given on the end of this form, together with further notes.

4. Give a full explanation of why each ground is being relied on:

....

....

....

....

Continue on a separate sheet if necessary:

Notes on the grounds for possession:

• If the court is satisfied that any of the grounds 1 to 8 are established, it must make an order (but see below in respect of fixed term tenancies).

• Before the court will grant an order on any of the grounds 9 to 17, it must be satisfied that it is reasonable to require you to leave. This means that, if one of these grounds is set out in section 3, you will be able to suggest to the court that it is not reasonable that you should have to leave, even if you accept that the ground applies.

• The court will not make an order under grounds 1, 3 to 7, 9 or 16 to take effect during the fixed term of the tenancy (if there is one) and it will only make an order during the fixed term on grounds 2, 8 or 10 to 15 or 17 if the terms of the tenancy make provision for it to be brought to an end on any of these grounds.

• Where the court makes an order for possession solely on ground 6 or 9, the landlord must pay your reasonable expenses.

5. Court Proceedings can not begin until after:

....

Date for court proceedings to commence:

....

• Where the landlord is seeking possession on grounds 1, 2, 5 to 7, 9 or 16, court proceedings cannot begin earlier than 2 months from the date this notice is served on you (even where one of grounds 3, 4, 8, 10 to 13, 14A, 15 or 17 is specified) and not before the date on which the tenancy (had it not been assured) could have been brought to an end by a notice to quit served at the same time as this notice.

• Where the landlord is seeking possession on grounds 3, 4, 8, 10 to 13, 14A, 15 or 17, court proceedings cannot begin earlier than 2 weeks from the date this notice is served (unless one of 1, 2, 5 or 7, 9 or 16 grounds is also specified in which case they cannot begin earlier than two months from the date this notice is served).

• Where the landlord is seeking possession on ground 14 (with or without other grounds), court proceedings cannot begin before the date this notice is served.

• Where the landlord s seeking possession on ground 14A, court proceedings cannot begin unless the landlord has served, or has taken all reasonable steps to serve, a copy of this notice on the partner who has left the property.

• After the date shown in section 4, court proceedings may be begun at once but not later than 12 months from the date on which this notice is served. After this time the notice will lapse and a new notice must be served before possession can be sought.

6. Name and address of landlord/licensor*:

To be signed and dated by the landlord or licensor or his or her agent (someone acting for him/her). If there are joint landlords or the agent must sign unless one signs on behalf of the rest with their agreement.

Full Name: ....

Address: ....

Postcode: ....

Telephone: (daytime) .... Evening ....

Email: ....

Address of Agent (if signed by agent): ....

....

Postcode: ....

Telephone: ....

Signed: .... **Date**: ....

Please cross out text marked with an asterisk (*) that does not apply.

Please specify whether:

Landlord*/licensor*/joint landlords*/landlord's agent*

What to do if this notice is served on you:

- This notice is the first step towards requiring you to give up possession of your home. You should read it carefully.

- Your landlord cannot make you leave your home without an order for possession issued by a court. By issuing this notice your landlord is informing you that he intends to seek such an order. If you are willing to give up possession without a court order, you should tell the person who signed this notice as soon as possible and say when you are prepared to leave.

- Whichever grounds are set out in section 3 of this form, the court may allow any of the other grounds to be added at a later date. If this is done, you will be told about it so you can discuss the additional grounds at the court hearing as well as the grounds set out in section 3.

- If you need advice about this notice, and what you should do about it, take it immediately to a citizens' advice bureau, a housing advice centre, a law centre or a solicitor.

Statutory Text to be used with Paragraph 3 - Grounds for Possession

In order to obtain possession of premises let under an Assured Tenancy Agreement, the landlord must specify a ground or grounds within the Housing Act 1988. With regard to Part I grounds, possession is compulsory. However, with regard to Part II grounds, it is up to the Court's discretion whether they will order possession for the landlord.

During the fixed term of an assured or shorthold tenancy, the landlord can only seek possession if one of grounds 2, 8, 10 to 15 or 17 apply and the terms of the tenancy make provision for it to be ended on any of these grounds: these grounds are marked with an asterisk (*) below.

When the fixed term of an assured tenancy ends, possession can be sought on any of the grounds. When the fixed term of a shorthold tenancy ends, the landlord does not have to give any grounds for possession.

A prior notice ground means that the landlord must have notified the tenant in writing before the tenancy started that he or she might seek possession on this ground.

Below is a full list of the grounds contained within the Act. Please use the statutory wording for the ground or grounds upon which you, as the landlord, are seeking possession of the premises.

Part I – MANDATORY GROUNDS
on which Court must Order Possession

Ground 1: Owner-occupier (a prior notice ground)

(Notice required: 2 months)

Not later than the beginning of the tenancy the landlord gave notice in writing to the tenant that possession might be recovered on this ground or the court is of the opinion that it is just and equitable to dispense with the requirement of notice and (in either case) (a) at some time before the beginning of the tenancy, the landlord who is seeking possession or, in the case of joint landlords seeking possession, at least one of them occupied the dwelling-house as his only or principal home; or (b) the landlord who is seeking possession or, in the case of joint landlords seeking possession, at least one of them requires the dwelling-house as his or his spouse's only or principal home and neither the landlord (or, in the case of joint landlords, any one of them) nor any other person who, as landlord, derived title under the landlord who gave the notice mentioned above acquired the reversion on the tenancy for money or money's worth.

Ground 2*: mortgagee (a prior notice ground)

(Notice required: 2 months)

The dwelling-house is subject to a mortgage granted before the beginning of the tenancy and (a) the mortgagee is entitled to exercise a power of sale conferred on him by the mortgage or by section 101 of the Law of Property Act 1925; and (b) the mortgagee requires possession of the dwelling-house for the purpose of disposing of it with vacant possession in exercise of that power; and

(c) either notice was given as mentioned in Ground 1 above or the court is satisfied that it is just and equitable to dispense with the requirement of notice; and for the purposes of this ground "mortgage" includes a charge and "mortgagee" shall be construed accordingly.

Ground 3: out of season holiday home (a prior notice ground)

(Notice required: 2 weeks)

The tenancy is a fixed term tenancy for a term not exceeding eight months and (a) not later than the beginning of the tenancy the landlord gave notice in writing to the tenant that possession might be recovered on this ground; and (b) at some time within the period of twelve months ending with the beginning of the tenancy, the dwelling-house was occupied under a right to occupy it for a holiday.

Ground 4: vacation let of educational accommodation (a prior notice ground)

(Notice required: 2 weeks)

The tenancy is a fixed term tenancy for a term not exceeding twelve months and (a) not later than the beginning of the tenancy the landlord gave notice in writing to the tenant that possession might be recovered on this ground; and (b) at some time within the period of twelve months ending with the beginning of the tenancy, the dwelling-house was let on a tenancy falling within paragraph 8 of Schedule 1 to this Act.

Ground 5: minister of religion (a prior notice ground)

(Notice required: 2 months)

The dwelling-house is held for the purpose of being available for occupation by a minister of religion as a residence from which to perform the duties of his office and (a) not later than the beginning of the tenancy the landlord gave notice in writing to the tenant that possession might be recovered on this ground; and (b) the court is satisfied that the dwelling-house is required for occupation by a minister of religion as such a residence.

Ground 6: demolition/reconstruction/substantial works

(Notice required: 2 months)

The landlord who is seeking possession or, if that landlord is a registered social landlord or charitable housing trust, a superior landlord intends to demolish or reconstruct the whole or a substantial part of the dwelling-house or to carry out substantial works on the dwelling-house or any part thereof or any building of which it forms part and the following conditions are fulfilled (a) the intended work cannot reasonably be carried out without the tenant giving up possession of the dwelling-house because (i) the tenant is not willing to agree to such a variation of the terms of the tenancy as would give such access and other facilities as would permit the intended work to be carried out, or (ii) the nature of the intended work is such that no such variation is practicable, or (iii) the tenant is not willing to accept an assured tenancy of such part only of the dwelling-house (in this sub-paragraph referred to as "the reduced part") as would leave in the possession of his landlord so much of the dwelling-house as would be reasonable to enable the intended work to be carried out and, where appropriate, as would give such access and other facilities over the reduced part as would permit the intended work to be carried out, or (iv) the nature of the intended work is such that such a tenancy is not practicable; and (b) either the landlord seeking possession acquired his interest in the dwelling-house before the grant of the tenancy or that interest was in existence at the time of that grant and neither that landlord (or, in the case of joint landlords, any of them) nor any other person who, alone or jointly with others, has acquired that interest since that time acquired it for money or money's worth; and (c) the assured tenancy on which the dwelling-house is let did not come into being by virtue of any provision of Schedule 1 to the Rent Act 1977, as amended by Part I of Schedule 4 to this Act or, as the case may be, section 4 of the Rent (Agriculture) Act 1976, as amended by Part II of that Schedule.

Ground 7: devolved tenancy

(Notice required: 2 months)

The tenancy is a periodic tenancy (including a statutory periodic tenancy) which has devolved under the will or intestacy of the former tenant and the proceedings for the recovery of possession are begun not later than twelve months after the death of the former tenant or, if the court so directs, after the date on which, in the opinion of the court, the landlord or, in the case of joint landlords, any one of them became aware of the former tenant's death. For the purposes of this ground, the acceptance by the landlord of rent from a new tenant after the death of the former tenant shall not be regarded as creating a new periodic tenancy, unless the landlord agrees in writing to a change (as compared with the tenancy before the death) in the amount of the rent, the period of the tenancy, the premises which are let or any other term of the tenancy.

Ground 8*: rent arrears

(Notice required: 2 weeks)

Both at the date of the service of the notice under section 8 of this Act relating to the proceedings for possession and at the date of the hearing (a) if rent is payable weekly or fortnightly, at least [eight weeks]' rent is unpaid; (b) if rent is payable monthly, at least [two months]' rent is unpaid; (c) if rent is payable quarterly, at least one quarter's rent is more than three months in arrears; and (d) if rent is payable yearly, at least three months' rent is more than three months in arrears; and for the purpose of this ground "rent" means rent lawfully due from the tenant.

Part II – DISCRETIONARY GROUNDS on which Court may Order Possession

Ground 9: suitable alternative accommodation

(Notice required: 2 months)

Suitable alternative accommodation is available for the tenant or will be available for him when the order for possession takes effect.

Ground 10*: rent arrears

(Notice required: 2 weeks)

Some rent lawfully due from the tenant (a) is unpaid on the date on which the proceedings for possession are begun; and (b) except where subsection (1)(b) of section 8 of this Act applies, was in arrears at the date of the service of the notice under that section relating to those proceedings.

Ground 11*: rent arrears

(Notice required: 2 weeks)

Whether or not any rent is in arrears on the date on which proceedings for possession are begun, the tenant has persistently delayed paying rent which has become lawfully due.

Ground 12*: breach

(Notice required: 2 weeks)

Any obligation of the tenancy (other than one related to the payment of rent) has been broken or not performed.

Ground 13*: condition of premises

(Notice required: 2 weeks)

The condition of the dwelling-house or any of the common parts has deteriorated owing to acts of waste by, or the neglect or default of, the tenant or any other person residing in the dwelling-house and, in the case of an act of waste by, or the neglect or default of, a person lodging with the tenant or a sub-tenant of his, the tenant has not taken such steps as he ought reasonably to have taken for the removal of the lodger or sub-tenant. For the purposes of this ground, "common parts" means any part of a building comprising the dwelling-house and any other premises which the tenant is entitled under the terms of the tenancy to use in common with the occupiers of other dwelling-houses in which the landlord has an estate or interest.

Ground 14*: nuisance

(Notice required: Immediately)

The tenant or a person residing in or visiting the dwelling-house (a) has been guilty of conduct causing or likely to cause a nuisance or annoyance to a person residing, visiting or otherwise engaging in a lawful activity in the locality, or (b) has been convicted of (i) using the dwelling-house or allowing it to be used for immoral or illegal purposes, or (ii) an arrestable offence committed in, or in the locality of, the dwelling-house.]

Ground 14A*: domestic violence

The dwelling-house was occupied (whether alone or with others) by a married couple or a couple living together as husband and wife and (a) one or both of the partners is a tenant of the dwelling-house, (b) the landlord who is seeking possession is a registered social landlord or a charitable housing trust, (c) one partner has left the dwelling-house because of violence or threats of violence by the other towards (i) that partner, or (ii) a member of the family of that partner who was residing with that partner immediately before the partner left, and (d) the court is satisfied that the partner who has left is unlikely to return.

Ground 15*: condition of furniture

(Notice required: 2 weeks)

The condition of any furniture provided for use under the tenancy has, in the opinion of the court, deteriorated owing to ill-treatment by the tenant or any other person residing in the dwelling-house and, in the case of ill-treatment by a person lodging with the tenant or by a sub-tenant of his, the tenant has not taken such steps as he ought reasonably to have taken for the removal of the lodger or sub-tenant.

Ground 16: employment

(Notice required: 2 months)

The dwelling-house was let to the tenant in consequence of his employment by the landlord seeking possession or a previous landlord under the tenancy and the tenant has ceased to be in that employment. [For the purposes of this ground, at a time when the landlord is or was the Secretary of State, employment by a health service body, as defined in section 60(7) of the National Health Service and Community Care Act 1990, shall be regarded as employment by the Secretary of State.]

Ground 17*: false statement

(Notice required: 2 weeks)

The tenant is the person, or one of the persons, to whom the tenancy was granted and the landlord was induced to grant the tenancy by a false statement made knowingly or recklessly by (a) the tenant, or (b) a person acting at the tenant's instigation.

Appendix IX

**Section 21 Notice
(Fixed Tenancy Period)
Requiring Possession of a Property**

SECTION 21 FIXED NOTICE

RECEIVED THIS....... DAY OF..................... 20......THE ORIGINAL NOTICE OF WHICH THIS IS A TRUE COPY

SIGNED ....

Housing Act 1988

Section 21(1) (b)

ASSURED SHORTHOLD TENANCY; NOTICE REQUIRING POSSESSION

FIXED TERM TENANCY

To: ....(name of tenant)

Of:...

....

....(address of tenant)

I/We* as/on behalf of* your landlord(s): ....

....(name of landlord)

Of:...

....

....(address of landlord)

GIVE YOU NOTICE THAT POSSESSION IS REQUIRED by virtue of Section 21(1) (b) of the Housing Act 1988 by me/ us/ your landlord(s)* of the premises:

....

....

....which you hold as tenant(s)

* On the .... day of ....

*at the end of the period of your tenancy which will end after the expiry of .... months from the service upon you of this Notice

Dated .... day of ....

Signed..

(name of agent) [to be completed by agent if serving notice]

....

(address of agent)..

....

....

INFORMATION FOR TENANT

1. If the tenant or licensee does not leave the dwelling, the landlord or licensor must get an order for possession from the court before the tenant or licensee can lawfully be evicted. The landlord or licensor cannot apply for such an order before the tenant or licensee can lawfully be evicted. The landlord or licensor cannot apply for such an order before the notice to quit or notice to determine has run out.

2. **A tenant or licensee who does not know if he has any right to remain in possession after a notice to quit or a notice to determine runs out can obtain advice from a solicitor. Help with all or part of the cost of legal advice and assistance may be available under the Legal Aid Scheme. He should also be able to obtain information from a Citizens' Advice Bureau, a Housing Aid Centre or a rent officer.**

Notes: Where an asterisk (*) is shown, delete the inapplicable alternative.

1. On or after the coming to an end of a fixed term assured shorthold tenancy, a court must make an order for possession if the landlord has given a notice in this form.

2. Where there are joint landlords, at least one of them must sign this notice.

3. This notice must (a) be served during the fixed term; (b) be given at least two calendar months before the fixed term is due to expire; and (c) cannot expire before the last day of the fixed term.

Appendix X

Section 21 Notice
(Periodic Tenancy)
Requiring Possession of a Property

SECTION 21 PERIODIC NOTICE

RECEIVED THIS .... DAY OF...................... 20... THE ORIGINAL NOTICE OF WHICH THIS IS A TRUE COPY

SIGNED...

Housing Act 1988

Section 21(4) (a)

ASSURED SHORTHOLD TENANCY; NOTICE REQUIRING POSSESSION

PERIODIC TENANCY

To: ....(name of tenant)

Of:...

....

....(address of tenant)

I/We* as/on behalf of* your landlord(s):..

....(name of landlord)

Of:...

....

....(address of landlord)

GIVE YOU NOTICE THAT POSSESSION IS REQUIRED by virtue of Section 21(1) (b) of the Housing Act 1988 by me/ us/ your landlord(s)* of the premises:

....

....which you hold as tenant(s)

* On the .... day of ....

*at the end of the period of your tenancy which will end after the expiry of
.... months from the service upon you of this Notice

Dated .... day of ....

Signed...

(name of agent) [to be completed by agent if serving notice]

....

(address of agent) ....

....

....

INFORMATION FOR TENANT

1. If the tenant or licensee does not leave the dwelling, the landlord or licensor must get an order for possession from the court before the tenant or licensee can lawfully be evicted. The landlord or licensor cannot apply for such an order before the tenant or licensee can lawfully be evicted. The landlord or licensor cannot apply for such an order before the notice to quit or notice to determine has run out.

2. **A tenant or licensee who does not know if he has any right to remain in possession after a notice to quit or a notice to determine runs out can obtain advice from a solicitor. Help with all or part of the cost of legal advice and assistance may be available under the Legal Aid Scheme. He should also be able to obtain information from a Citizens' Advice Bureau, a Housing Aid Centre or a rent officer.**

Notes: Where an asterisk (*) is shown, delete the inapplicable alternative.

1. Where an assured shorthold tenancy is a periodic tenancy, a court must make an order for possession if the landlord has given a notice in this form.

2. Where there are joint landlords, at least one of them must sign this notice.

3. This notice must expire: (a) on the last day of a period of the tenancy; (b) AND at least two calendar months after this notice is given.

Epilogue

This book was conceived of a desire to give form to an entity through which I could not only share the secrets of my success in property but also inspire readers to become the best that you can be.

With so much important and exciting information that I needed to share with readers about how to become a truly successful property investor, it was difficult to cram all this information into one book! Along with many property investors and other entrepreneurs I meet, I am passionate about self-development and mindset as well as property; but being determined to focus on giving solid practical information about property investing, I have only lightly touched upon these other aspects in the book that I believe are integral to success in any sphere.

I hope some of you will want to continue the relationship we embark on as you read this book, by visiting my website at www.propertyinvestingsuccess.co.uk where you can keep up-to-date with the latest property investing news and techniques; as well as more about about self-development, networking opportunities and developing multiple streams of income.

I would love to hear from you after reading the book, particularly about how it has helped you to achieve success in property. You can contact me at angela@propertyinvestingsuccess.co.uk.